BIBLE STUDY COURSE
NEW TESTAMENT

THE DALLAS HIGH SCHOOLS
SEPTEMBER, 1946

BULLETIN NO. 170
AUTHORIZED BY BOARD OF EDUCATION
APRIL 23, 1946

PRINTED IN
THE DALLAS PUBLIC SCHOOLS PRINTSHOP
DALLAS, TEXAS

—1381—46

Reprinted in 1993 by WallBuilders, Inc.

For additional copies of this book, for information on other books, or to arrange for presentations of this material to groups, write WallBuilders, P.O. Box 397, Aledo, Texas, 76008-0397, (817) 441-6044.

Published by:

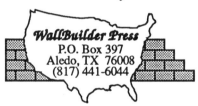

WallBuilder Press
P.O. Box 397
Aledo, TX 76008
(817) 441-6044

Printed in the United States of America

ISBN 0-925279-28-5

FOREWORD

For a number of years the Dallas public schools allowed one-half credit toward high-school graduation for the successful completion of a general survey course in the Bible, given in the churches and Sunday schools of the city. In 1939, it was decided to provide separate courses in the Old and the New Testaments, each course carrying one-half unit of credit toward high-school graduation.

In both the Old Testament and the New Testament study courses an attempt has been made to avoid controversial questions by placing emphasis on the study of the Bible itself. Standards of work and teaching procedures are expected to approximate as closely as possible those used in the day schools.

Grateful acknowledgement is made to all teachers of the Bible-study classes who have helped either by suggestions or committee work to prepare this revised New Testament Study Course.

We wish to give special credit to Miss Onie B. Easley, teacher of English in N. R. Crozier Technical High School and to Miss Jessie Hawkins, teacher in John H. Brown Elementary School for their many contributions and their valuable assistance in editing the manuscript.

E. B. COMSTOCK,
Assistant Superintendant
in Charge of High Schools

CONTENTS

v

THE BIBLE

Born in the East and clothed in Oriental form and imagery, the Bible walks the ways of the world with familiar feet and enters land after land to find its own everywhere. It has learned to speak in hundreds of languages to the hearts of men. It comes into the palace to tell the monarch that he is a servant of the Most High, and into the cottage to assure the peasant that he is a son of God. Children listen to its stories with wonder and delight, and wise men ponder them as parables of life. It has a word of peace for the time of peril, a word of comfort for the time of calamity, a word of light for the hour of darkness. Its oracles are repeated in the assembly of the people, and its counsels whispered in the ear of the lonely. The wicked and the proud tremble at its warnings, but to the wounded and the penitent it has a mother's voice. The wilderness and the solitary place have been made glad by it, and the fire on the hearth has lit the reading of its wellworn page. It has woven itself into our dearest dreams; so that love, friendship, sympathy and devotion, memory and hope, put on the beautiful garments of its treasured speech, breathing of frankincense and myrrh. No man is poor or desolate who has this treasure for his own. When the landscape darkens and the trembling pilgrim comes to the Valley named of the Shadow, he is not afraid to enter; he takes the rod and staff of scripture in his hand; he says to friend and comrade; "Good-bye, we shall meet again." and comforted by that support, he goes toward the lonely pass as one who walks through darkness into light.

Henry Van Dyke.

INTRODUCTION

REGULATIONS GOVERNING
NEW TESTAMENT STUDY COURSE

1. Classes may be organized by any Sunday school or church or any other religious organization for the purpose of studying the Bible in their respective organizations with a view to obtaining high-school credit. Successful completion of the course gives one-half unit of credit toward high-school graduation.

2. An application blank, giving necessary information about the class, must be filled out and filed with the Assistant Superintendent in charge of Dallas High Schools.

3. There must be a minimum of forty class periods of 90 minutes net teaching time; or sixty 60-minute periods, net time; or eighty 45-minute periods, net time. *In no case will fewer than forty different class sessions be accepted.*

4. The text used is the NEW TESTAMENT STUDY COURSE, a syllabus published by the authority of the Dallas Board of Education for use in Bible study credit classes.

5. The teacher must have a minimum preparation of at least a high-school education, and sufficient teaching experience or training in Bible Study to warrant success in teaching the Bible course.

6. Accurate record of attendance and date of class meetings must be kept. Pupils are expected to make up for all lesson periods missed. Pupils with excessive or unexcused absence record will not be permitted to take the final examination.

7. The New Testament course is opened to second-, third-, and fourth-year high school pupils (10th, 11th, and 12th year pupils). It is highly desirable, but not required, that the Old Testament course be completed before the New Testament course is begun.

8. All pupils who desire credit must pass an examination held under the auspices of the Board of Education. This examination will be at the close of the school year or at some other approved time. Final examination questions will be based on the text used—NEW TESTAMENT STUDY COURSE.

9. Before a pupil is eligible to take an examination for credit in Bible, certification of his having fulfilled the necessary requirements, both as to work and attendance, must be made by his Sunday school superintendent and teacher. Suitable forms for this purpose are supplied by the Superintendent of the City Schools.

MINIMUM REQUIREMENTS
(NEW TESTAMENT)

The course is itself a "minimum course," since teachers are expected to supplement rather than subtract from the topics included. The following summary requirements are listed for purpose of emphasis and review:

1. Ability to name and classify the books of the Bible (common classification).

2. General knowledge of the New Testament as outlined in the course of study. Reading of the entire New Testament is required.

3. Ability to reproduce the memory passages indicated in connection with the lessons and given in full in the appendix.

4. Ability to identify or complete designated quotations.

5. Ability to define the following terms: Bible, gospel, testament, advocate, disciple, ordinance, transfiguration, temple, synagogue, miracle, parable, gentile, publican, sanhedrin, leper, alms, beatitude, scribes, Pharisees, Sadducees. (For definition of these terms, see "Glossary" in the Appendix.)

6. Familiarity with the following Bible characters: Jesus, John Baptist, Mary, Elizabeth, Martha, Matthew, Mark, Luke, John, Nicodemus, Pilate, Judas Iscariot, Thomas, Peter, Stephen, Philip, Barnabas, Paul, Timothy, James, Titus.

7. Knowledge of the political divisions and geography of New Testament Palestine:

    a. Ability to make a sketch map of Palestine showing the three main political divisions, the Jordan River, the Sea of Galilee, the Dead Sea, Jerusalem, Bethlehem, Nazareth, Jericho, Capernaum, Mt. Herman, Mt. of Olives.

    b. Familiarity with following additional geographical features:

        (1) **Places:** Bethany, Hebron, Antioch, Joppa, Tyre, Damascus, Ephesus, Phillippi, Corinth, Athens, Rome.

        (2) **Countries and Provinces:** Perea, Phoenicia, Decapolis, Asia Minor, Greece, Italy.

8. Ability to use a concordance and other reference books.

9. Regular attendance upon class meetings, and consistent class work. All absences from class meetings must be made up by special meetings or examinations over the work missed, as in the day school. The responsibility of making up work missed should rest largely on the pupil. Excessive absence and unexcused absences will result in failure to receive credit.

10. Fair knowledge of the course, and ability to make a grade of E (70) or above, on the final examination.

EVENTS BETWEEN
THE OLD AND NEW TESTAMENTS

Prophetic Silence. The writings of the Old Testament closed with the prophecy of Malachi, who was contemporary with Ezra and Nehemiah, about 432 B.C. Thus from Malachi to the beginning of the New Testament, a period of a little more than 400 years, no inspired writer appeared. This period is very appropriately called the "Period of Prophetic Silence."

For facts relating to the Jews during this time, reliance must be placed upon Greek and Latin historians, Josephus and books of the Apocrypha (books usually regarded by Protestants as uninspired).

The Political Situation. During the period between the Old and the New Testaments, Judah was ruled by Persia for about 100 years. It was then governed more than 100 years by Greece, during which time the Grecian language became universal. After this, Judah was under the control of Syrian kings for some thirty-nine years. Then came the period of the Maccabees, Jewish leaders who successfully revolted against the Syrians and thus regained for the Jews national independence which lasted for a period of about 100 years. In 64 B.C., Rome came into possession of Palestine. The Jews were required to pay tribute to Caesar, but were granted full religious rights, still under the leadership of the Maccabees. When Herod was made ruler of Judea by the Romans in 47 B.C., he suppressed the last of the Maccabees and the Jews again lost their independence.

Religious Sects and Parties. During this interim before the birth of Christ several religious parties, or sects, had developed, among which the most prominent were the Pharisees, the Sadducees, the Essenes, and the Herodians (the latter being more political than religious). They were all comparatively small in numbers but exercised great influence among the people. The largest and most prominent of these religious sects was the Pharisees. Their teachings appealed to the people and finally gained for them the control of the temple. They were extremely conservative and very punctilious in the observance of the Jewish traditions and ceremonies. They believed in angels, spirits, future life or immortality, and in the freedom of the will. At the time of Christ they had become very largely mere legalists or formalists, observing the letter of the law but disregarding the real spirit of the commandments. They were, consequently, many times the victims of Christ's bitter denunciations for their hypocritical and self-righteous attitude.

Of almost equal prominence with the Pharisees were the Sadducees, a small but wealthy and influential group composed largely of the priestly aristocracy. They were liberals and free thinkers and bitter opponents of the Pharisees. They held a negative attitude toward religious questions and rejected the traditions of the elders. They did not believe in angels or spirits or a future life. They held places on the high religious court, the Sanhedrin, and were constantly interested in maintaining their privileged position.

The Essenes comprised a more or less secret society composed of individuals and brotherhoods, and occupied an intermediate position between the Pharisees and the Sadducees. They practiced voluntary poverty and held in common much of their goods. They were opposed to slavery, despised pleasure and luxury, wore simple clothing, and ate simple food. They prided themselves in being ascetic, holding pain and the ordinary miseries of life to be of little consequence. They regarded the control of the passions as a chief virtue. They were devout and held prayers before meals and before sundown. They were initiated into their order by taking an oath of secrecy. Many of them practiced celibacy and became the forerunners of the subsequent orders of nuns, monks, hermits, and frairs. Mention of the Essenes is not found in the New Testament.

The Herodians constituted a political party rather than a religious order among the Jews. The name was derived from the support given by members of the party from the dynasty of Herod. The Herodians had little in common with other parties or sects except opposition to the work and teachings of Jesus.

The Samaritans. The Samaritans were neither a political nor a religious sect. They were a mixed people resulting chiefly from the intermarriage of Babylonian colonists who were sent to Samaria after the captivity of the northern tribes, or Israelites, with the remnant of the poor and weak Jews who were not carried off to foreign lands. The name *Samaritans* was applied to this people after the name of the country or the capital city, Samaria. They did not worship at the temple in Jerusalem but established a rival worship at

Mt. Gerizim where their temple was located. Orthodox Jews despised the Samaritans and had little dealings with them.

The Synagogue. The term *synagogue* is generally used to designate a place of Jewish worship or religious instruction. The synagogue probably had its origin in the circumstances confronting the Hebrews while in exile. These people could not, in a strange land, offer sacrifices as they had done in their home country; but they could meet together and hear the law and the prophets read. In the gatherings held in the home of Ezekiel may be found, some believe, the germ of the future Synagogue (Ezekiel 8:20). After the return from the Exile, if not before, synogogues were established in Palestine. It is known from old sources that synagogues were established by the dispersed Jews in Egypt.

Some authorities believe that the institution of the synagogue grew up along with the temple and developed from it. The synagogue had its most rapid development during the age of the Maccabees. At the time of Christ synagogues existed throughout Palestine and in most parts of the Roman Empire. The chief officer, usually a rabbi, was called the ruler of the synagogue; next in order were the elders or heads of the synagogues. The early Christians used the synagogues as opportune places for proclaiming the gospel of Christ. Synagogues served not only as houses of prayer or places of religious worship but also as assembly places, law courts, and schools for both religious and secular instruction. The synagogue occupied then, and does now, a most important place among the Jewish people, and was the center of their religious and social life.

World Conditions at the Birth of Christ. At the time Jesus was born, world conditions were particularly suitable for the spread of a new faith. The world was under the rule of the Roman Empire. The Greek language was universally used and understood. Transportation from place to place in the Empire was comparatively swift and sure, by boat, well-made roads, and everywhere travelers were under the protection of a trained soldiery. The Jewish people, finding it impossible to regain their complete national independence, had turned their attention to matters of religious controversy. Sects such as the Pharisees and Saducees and secret societies like the Essenes had come into prominence. There was a general feeling of expectation among devout Jews that God would visit and deliver His people.

SUGGESTIONS TO TEACHERS

The following brief suggestions are offered for the help of teachers:

1. Members of the Bible study classes should be impressed at the outset with the value of a knowledge of the Bible, both from a cultural and personal point of view.

2. The teacher should make sure that all members of the class understand clearly the regulations governing credit in this course, as explained on page v.

3. In general, the arrangement of the lesson topics given in the syllabus should be followed. Supplementary topics and review lessons may be added at the discretion of the teacher.

4. The amount of time to be devoted to the different lessons is intended to be suggestive. It is necessary, however, for the teacher who deviates from the printed lesson arrangement to make a careful estimate of the time required to complete the course.

5. Pupils should be required to keep systematically some kind of notebook, containing special readings and outlines, special assignments, quotations, memory passages, sketch maps, and such other items as the teacher may see fit to have included in the notebook.

6. Careful study should be given to the geography of Palestine and to the manners and customs of the times. All pupils should be familiar with the map of Palestine and should be able to draw a sketch map showing the main divisions of Palestine during the time of Christ.

7. Systematic attention should be given to the study of quotations and memory passages in connection with each lesson.

8. It is highly desirable that the teacher and the class possess needed supplementary materials and aids, such as charts and reference books. Pupils should be encouraged to make certain illustrative materials for class demonstrations.

9. Careful attention should be given to oral and written tests in connection with each class period. Occasionally full period reviews and written tests should be given, as in the day school. Pupils may be asked to formulate original questions, participate in memory contests, spelling and matching contests, make-believe radio contests, etc.

10. The teaching procedure should be varied according to the nature of the lesson, the maturity and ability of the pupils, the size of the class, and other factors.

BIBLE STUDY COURSE
NEW TESTAMENT

PART ONE
THE LIFE AND MINISTRY OF CHRIST

INTRODUCTION

The one hundred eighty-two events in the life of Christ, which are included in this outline, are arranged chronologically. The references include a harmony of the four books of the gospel. Since the gospel according to Luke is more chronologically written than any one of the others it has been used, quite extensively.

Matthew, Mark, and Luke are known as books of the *Synoptic gospels*—meaning seen together. Matthew was a Jew writing to the Jews. He was interested in portraying Christ as the Messiah of the Jews. Mark was a Jew writing to the Romans. He relates the active ministry of Jesus. Luke was a Greek. He supplies some incidents that are passed over by the other three gospel writers. John was a Jew writing to all peoples. He tells us his purpose in John 20:31—" that ye might believe that Jesus is the Christ, the Son of God." Mark was written about 50 A.D., Matthew about 60 A.D., Luke about 70 A.D., and John about 90 A.D. The exact date and order of these books is unknown.

A careful reading of each gospel will be profitable in order to get the style and purpose of each author as he tells the story of Christ.

Lesson I

I. The Birth and Childhood of Christ

*1. The pre-existence of Christ
    John 1:1-14.**

2. The genealogies
    Matthew 1:1-17.** Luke 3:23-38.**

---

* The starred (*) events are to be stressed.
** The basic references for this course are double-starred. Pupils should read all references, individually or cooperatively.

[3]

3. The birth of John the Baptist foretold to Zacharias in the Temple
   Luke 1:5-25.**

*4. The annunciation of the birth of Christ to Mary at Nazareth
   Luke 1:26-38.**

5. The visit of Mary to Elizabeth; greetings and songs exchanged
   Luke 1:39-56.**

6. The birth and childhood of John the Baptist in Judea
   Luke 1:57-80.**

7. The announcement to Joseph of the approaching birth of Jesus
   Matthew 1:18-25.**

*8. The birth of Jesus in Bethlehem
   Luke 2:1-20.**

9. The circumcision of Jesus, naming, presentation in Temple
   Luke 2:21-39.**

10. The visit of the wise men from the East to Jerusalem and Bethlehem
    Matthew 2:1-12.**

11. The flight into Egypt and return to Nazareth
    Matthew 2:13-23.**

*12. The childhood and youth of Jesus at Nazareth
    Luke 2:40,** 51-52.**

*13. The visit of Jesus to Jerusalem at the age of twelve
    Luke 2:41-50.**

NOTE: Teachers will prefer to make their own questions on most topics. However, it is thought that the questions given in connection with some of the topics will prove helpful as teaching devices. They are intended to emphasize some of the outstanding events in the life of Christ, to call special attention to some of the interesting details, and to serve as aids to a better understanding and appreciation of the teachings of Christ.

Questions—Lesson I.

The Pre-existence of Christ (John 1:1-14)

1. Where was Christ before he was born on earth? (1, 2, 14)
2. What titles does John apply to Christ in this chapter? (1, 4, 5, 9, 14)
3. For what purpose was John sent by God? (7, 8)

The Annunciation, Birth, and Infancy of Jesus (Luke 1:26-2:38; Matthew 1:18-2:20)

1. Name five things the angel told Mary concerning her child Jesus. (32, 33)
2. What does the word "Jesus" mean? (Salvation of Jehovah)
3. How did the angel explain the miraculous births of John and Jesus? (37)
4. Why were Joseph and Mary in Bethlehem when Jesus was born? (Luke 2:1-5)
5. What were the good tidings brought to the shepherds by the angel? (11)
6. Who accompanied the angel, and what were they saying? (13, 14)
7. How were the shepherds to recognize the baby Jesus? (12)
8. What did they do when they had seen Jesus? (17, 20)
9. Why was Herod troubled? (Matthew 2:2, 3)
10. How were the wise men guided to the child? (9)
11. Why did they not return to Herod as he had requested them to do? (12)
12. Why did Joseph take Mary and the child into Egypt? (13)
13. How long did they remain in Egypt? (15)
14. What did Herod do when the wisemen failed to return to him? (16)
15. Why did Joseph take Jesus and the mother out of Egypt? (19, 20)
16. Where did he take them and why? (21-23)

His Childhood and Youth at Nazareth (Luke 2:40-52)

17. Verses 40, 51, 52 contain a summary of the life of Christ

from infancy to the age of about thirty. What do they tell about him?

18. The only recorded incident of these years is related in verses 42-49. What was it? What astonished the people who heard him in the Temple? (47) What was his answer to his mother's question concerning his actions? (49)

Memorize:

The pre-existence of Christ:

"In the beginning was the Word, and the Word was with God, and the Word was God . . . All things were made by him; and without him was not anything made that was made . . . And the Word was made flesh, and dwelt among us, (and we beheld his glory, and the glory as of the only begotten of the Father,) full of grace and truth." John 11, 3, 14.

Quotations for careful study:[1]

First mention of Christ: "And God said, 'Let us make man in our image, after our likeness.'" Genesis 1:26.

First promise concerning Christ: "And I will put enmity between thee and the woman, and between thy seed and her seed; it shall bruise thy head, and thou shalt bruise his heel." Genesis 3:15.

Isaiah's prophecy about Christ: "He was numbered with the transgressors; and he bare the sin of many, and made intercession for the transgressors." Isaiah 53:12.

"Glory to God in the highest, and on earth, peace, good will toward men." Luke 2:14.

"Know ye not that I must be about my Father's business?" Luke 2:49.

   . . . .

Locate Bethlehem, Jerusalem, and Nazareth.

Explain the following terms: *Bible, Immanuel, Jesus, Temple*[2].

Identify the following: John the Baptist, Zacharias, Elizabeth, Mary, Joseph, Gabriel, Wise Men, shepherds, Herod, Anna, Simeon.

---

[1]The quotations given in connection with each lesson, together with others selected by the teacher or the pupil, are to be written in the pupil's notebook, with such explanations or comment as will make the setting and meaning clear. Usually the pupil should write the name of the speaker, the one spoken to and the purpose of the speaker or the condition under which the message was spoken.

[2]See the Glossary.

Lesson II

II. The Preparation of Christ for His Public Ministry

*14. The preaching of John in Judea
Matthew 3:1-12. Mark 1:1-8. Luke 3:1-18.**

*15. The Baptism of Jesus by John in the Jordan
Matthew 3:13-17. Mark 1:9-11. Luke 3:21-23.**

*16. The temptation of Jesus in the wilderness
Matthew 4:1-11. Mark 1:12-13. Luke 4:1-13.**

*17. The testimony of John the Baptist concerning Jesus
John 1:19-34.**

Questions—Lesson II.

His Baptism and His Temptation (Luke 3:21-23; 4:1-13)

1. Where did John preach, and what did he preach? (Luke 3:3)
2. Why did he preach? (Luke 3:2, 4)
3. Where did Jesus go when he left Nazareth, and for what purpose? (Mark 1:9)
4. What supernatural events followed the baptism of Jesus? (Luke 3:21, 22)
5. Why did Jesus go into the Wilderness? (Luke 4:1; Matthew 4:1)
6. Relate the first temptation and how Jesus met it; the second; the third. (According to Luke's account; Luke 4:1-13) What weapon did Christ use to defend himself in this conflict with the devil?

The Testimony of John Concerning Jesus (John 1:19-34)

7. Who did John tell the priests and Levites he was? (23)
8. What testimony did John give concerning Jesus? (32-34)
9. What was the sign by which John identified Jesus as the Messiah? (33)

Memorize:

Jesus to the devil in the wilderness: "It is written, Man shall not live by bread alone, but by every word that proceedeth out of the mouth of God . . . It is written again, Thou

---

* The starred (*) events are to be stressed.
** The basic references for this course are double-starred. Pupils should read all references, individually or cooperatively.

shalt not tempt the Lord thy God . . . Get thee hence, Satan:
for it is written, Thou shalt worship the Lord thy God, and
him only shalt thou serve." Matthew 4:4, 7, 10.

Quotations for careful study:

John announces his office: "I am the voice of one crying
in the wilderness, 'Make straight the way of the Lord, as
said the prophet Esaias.'" John 1:23.

John's testimony concerning Jesus: "The latchet of whose
shoes I am not worthy to unloose." Mark 1:7.

. . . .

Locate the Jordan River.

Explain the following terms: *Gospel and synagogue.*

Lesson III

III. The Early Ministry of Christ

18. The calling of the first disciples
    John 1:35-51.**

*19. The first miracle—water made into wine at Cana; residence
    changed from Nazareth to Capernaum
    John 2:1-11.** 2:12.

20. The first cleansing of the Temple on the day of the
    Passover
    John 2:13-22.**

21. The miracles in Jerusalem where many believed
    John 2:23-25.**

*22. The first recorded discourse to Nicodemus on the New
    Birth
    John 3:1-21.**

23. The ministry of Jesus in Judea and further testimony
    by John
    John 3:22-36.**

24. The first converts in Samaria at Jacob's Well
    John 4:1-42.**

25. The reception by the Galileans—the second miracle at
    Cana, the Nobleman's son
    Matthew 4:12. John 4:43-54.**

26. The imprisonment of John the Baptist by Herod
    Luke 3:19-20.**

27. The beginning of Christ's Galilean ministry
    Matthew 4:17. Mark 1:14-15. Luke 4:14-15.**

28. The rejection of Jesus as Messiah at Nazareth (First?)
    Luke 4:16-30.**

29. The moving of His residence to Capernaum
    Matthew 4:13-16. 4:31.**

Questions—Lesson III.

The First Recorded Discourse of Jesus (John 3:1-21)

1. To whom? What was the subject? Who was Nicodemus?
2. How did Nicodemus say he knew that Jesus was a teacher from God? (2)
3. What did Jesus say to him? (3) Did he understand what Jesus meant? (4)
4. How did Jesus explain the birth of the Spirit? (6, 8)
5. Was the principal object of Christ's coming salvation, or judgment? (17)
6. Is judgment an inevitable result? (18)
7. Why did men love darkness rather than light? (19)

Memorize:

The purpose of Christ's coming: "For God so loved the world, that he gave his only begotten Son, that whosoever believeth in him should not perish, but have eternal life." John 3:16.

Quotations for careful study:

Necessity of a new birth: "Marvel not that I say unto thee, thou must be born again." John 3:7.

"God is a spirit; and they that worship Him must worship Him in spirit and in truth." John 4:24.

Doing the Father's will: "My meat is to do the will of Him that sent me, and to finish His work." John 4:34.

· · · · · · · ·

Locate Cana, Sychar, Capernaum, and Bethsaida.

---

* The starred (*) events are to be stressed.
** The basic references for this course are double-starred. Pupils should read all references, individually or cooperatively.

Explain the following terms: *miracle, worship, discourse,* and *Passover.*

Identify Peter, Andrew, Philip, and Nathaniel.

Lesson IV

IV. The Great Galilean Ministry of Christ

*30. The calling of the first disciples to follow Him—four fishermen
   Matthew 4:18-22.   Mark 1:16-20.   Luke 5:1-11.**

31. The healing of the demoniac in the synagogue at Capernaum
   Mark 1:21-28.   Luke 4:31-37.**

32. The healing of Peter's wife's mother and many others in Capernaum and Galilee
   Matthew 8:14-17.   Mark 1:29-34.   Luke 4:38-41.**

33. The preaching tour through Galilee
   Matthew 4:23-25.   Mark 1:35-39.   Luke 4:42-44.**

34. The healing of a leper which arouses much interest, attracts multitudes, and causes retirement to the wilderness
   Matthew 8:2-4   Mark 1:40-45   Luke 5:12-16**

35. The healing of the paralytic let down through the roof at Capernaum (Beginning of open opposition by scribes and Pharisees)
   Matthew 9:2-8.   Mark 2:1-12.   Luke 5:17-26.**

36. The calling of Matthew
   Matthew 9:9.   Mark 2:13-14.   Luke 5:27-28.**

37. The healing of the man at the Pool of Bethesda, in Jerusalem on the Sabbath; accusation against Him; His defense
   John 5:1-47.**

38. The defending of the disciples who pluck grain on the Sabbath
   Matthew 12:1-8.   Mark 2:23-28.   Luke 6:1-5.**

39. The defending of the healing of the withered hand on the Sabbath
   Matthew 12:9-13.   Mark 3:1-6.   Luke 6:6-11.**

40. The healing of multitudes by the sea of Galilee
    Matthew 12:14-21.** Mark 3:7-12.

*41. The selecting of the twelve apostles
    Matthew 10:2-4. Mark 3:13-19. Luke 6:12-16.**

Questions—Lesson IV.

The Selection of the Twelve Apostles   (Luke 6:12-16; Mark 3:13-19)

1. Where was Jesus and what did he do the night before he chose his apostles? (Luke 6:12)
2. For what purpose were they chosen? (Mark 3:14, 15)
3. Name the twelve. (16-19)

Memorize:
Jesus reproves the Pharisees for their ignorance of the Scriptures. "Search the scriptures; for in them ye think ye have eternal life: and they are they which testify of me." John 5:39.

Quotations for careful study:
"The Son of man hath power on earth to forgive sins." Matthew 9:6.
"Come ye after me, and I will make you to become fishers of men." Mark 1:17.

. . . .

Locate the Sea of Galilee and the Pool of Bethesda.

Explain the following terms: *disciple, publican, tradition, leper, appoint, apostle,* and *impotent.*

Lesson V

The Great Galilean Ministry of Christ (continued)

*42. The Sermon on the Mount
    Matthew 5-7. Luke 6:17-49

    (1) The introduction and beatitudes
        Matthew 5:1-12.**

    (2) The influence of His followers—salt, light
        Matthew 5:13-26.**

---

* The starred (*) events are to be stressed.
** The basic references for this course are double-starred. Pupils should read all references, individually or cooperatively.

    (3) The relation of Christ's teaching to that of Old Testament and tradition
Matthew 5:17-48.**

    (4) The teaching concerning almsgiving, prayer, and fasting
Matthew 6:1-18.**

    (5) The teaching concerning laying up treasures and worldy anxiety
Matthew 6:19-34.**

    (6) The teaching concerning judgment
Matthew 7:1-6.**

    (7) The teaching concerning prayer
Matthew 7:7-11.**

    (8) The Golden Rule
Matthew 7:12.**

    (9) The two ways
Matthew 7:13-14.**

   (10) The false prophets
Matthew 7:15-23.**

   (11) The conclusion and application (two builders) and effect
Matthew 7:24-29.**

Questions—Lesson V.

The Sermon on the Mount   (Matthew, Chapters 5, 6, 7)

1. Were the beatitudes what the leaders of Israel would expect to hear? Why?

2. What two metaphors did Jesus use to name the influence of His followers? (5:13-14)

3. Did Christ recognize the Law of Moses as a God-given covenant? What did He say His relation to it was? (5:17)

4. What does the Sermon teach concerning reconciliation? 5:23, 24) Concerning divorce? (5:32) Concerning forswearing? (5:33-37) Retaliation? (5:39-41)

5. Under the old law, one was allowed to return for an injury a like injury. Do you think the purpose of this law was to teach the offended that vengeance was right, or to

teach the offender the consequences of offending? Give reasons.

6. What did Christ teach in the Sermon about lending and giving? (5:42)

7. How should we treat our enemies? (5:44) Why? (5:45)

8. Who should be our ideal and model in perfectness? (5:48)

9. What is the reward of hypocrites and why? (6:2) Does Jesus forbid public giving, or only the spirit that desires publicity? Give reasons for your answer.

10. Why did the Pharisees like to pray? (5) Did Jesus forbid public prayer? Why is it necessary for us to forgive those who trespass against us? (6:15)

11. What are Christ's instructions concerning fasting? (6:16-18)

12. What did Christ command concerning laying up of treasures? (6:19-21) Is it wrong, then, to have wordly treasures?

13. What must we seek above all else? (6:33)

14. What did Christ teach concerning judging? (7:1-5)

15. What was His teaching concerning prayer? (7:7; 7-11; 6:9-13)

16. Name the two ways and give the contrast drawn by Jesus between them. (7:13-14)

17. How are false prophets to be recognized? (7:16)

18. Explain the similes used by Christ in concluding His Sermon. (7:24-29)

19. What effect did His teachings have upon the people and why? (7:28-29)

Memorize:
BEATITUDES
"Blessed are the poor in spirit: for theirs is the kingdom of heaven.

"Blessed are they that mourn: for they shall be comforted.

"Blessed are the meek: for the shall inherit the earth.

"Blessed are they which do hunger and thirst after righteousness: for they shall be filled.

"Blessed are the merciful: for they shall obtain mercy.

"Blessed are the pure in heart: for they shall see God.

"Blessed are the peacemakers: for they shall be called the children of God.

"Blessed are they which are persecuted for righteousness' sake: for theirs is the kingdom of heaven.

"Blessed are ye, when men shall revile you, and persecute you, and shall say all manner of evil against you falsely, for my sake.

"Rejoice and be exceeding glad: for great is your reward in heaven: for so persecuted they the prophets which were before you." Matthew 5:3-12.

THE LORD'S PRAYER

"Our Father which art in heaven, Hallowed be thy name.

"Thy kingdom come. Thy will be done in earth, as it is in heaven.

"Give us this day our daily bread.

"And forgive us our debts, as we forgive our debtors.

"And lead us not into temptation, but deliver us from evil:

"For thine is the kingdom, and the power, and the glory, forever. Amen." Matthew 6:9-13.

THE GOLDEN RULE

"Therefore all things whatsoever ye would that men should do to you, do ye even so to them: for this is the law and the prophets." Matthew 7:12.

What shall we seek above all else?

"But seek ye first the kingdom of God, and his righteousness; and all these things shall be added unto you." Matthew 6:33.

The three-fold promise of prayer:

"Ask, and it shall be given you; seek, and ye shall find; knock, and it shall be opened unto you." Matthew 7:7.

Quotations for careful study:

A metaphor Jesus used to show the influence of his followers: "Ye are the salt of the earth." Matthew 5:13.

A metaphor Jesus used to show the influence of his followers: "Ye are the light of the world." Matthew 5:16.

"For where your treasure is, there will your heart be also." Matthew 6:21.

"Judge not, that ye be not judged." Matthew 7:1.

"By their fruits ye shall know them." Matthew 7:20.

"For He taught them as one having authority, and not as the scribes." Matthew 7:49.

Lesson VI

The Great Galilean Ministry of Christ (continued)

43. The healing of the Centurion's servant at Capernaum
    Matthew 8:5-13. Luke 7:1-10.**

44. The raising of the widow's son
    Luke 7:11-17.**

45. The inquiry of John the Baptist who is in prison and the answers of Jesus
    Matthew 11:2-19. Luke 7:18-23.**

46. The bearing witness to John's character and ministry
    Luke 7:24-35.**

47. The reproving of cities, prayer of thanksgiving, invitation to the weary
    Matthew 11:20-30.**

48. The anointing by a sinful woman
    Luke 7:36-50.**

49. Another tour of Galilee
    Luke 8:1-3.**

50. The blasphemous accusations of the Jews
    Matthew 12:22-37. Mark 3:20-30. Luke 11:14-23.**

51. The reproving of the scribes and Pharisees for seeking for a sign
    Matthew 12:38-45. Luke 11:29-36.**

52. The teaching regarding His Mother and brethren
    Matthew 12:46-50. Mark 3:31-35. Luke 8:19-21.**

*53. The teaching in parables by the Sea of Galilee
    Matthew 13:1-53.** Mark 4:1-34. Luke 8:4-18.

Questions—Lesson VI.

1. Where did Jesus go after preaching the Sermon on the Mount? (Luke 7:1)

---

* The starred (*) events are to be stressed.
** The basic references for this course are double-starred. Pupils should read all references, individually or cooperatively.

2. Why did the Centurion not want Jesus to enter his home? (Luke 7:6)

3. What great miracle did Jesus perform at Nain? (Luke 7:12.)

4. What effect did this miracle have upon the people, and what did they think about Jesus? (Luke 7:16)

5. A deputation from John the Baptist came to Jesus with what question? (Luke 7:19)

6. What was Jesus' reply to John's question? (Luke 7:22)

7. Quote Jesus as to his estimate of John's ministry and his character. (Luke 7:24-30)

8. Why did Jesus reprove the cities where his mighty work had been done? (Matthew 11:20-21)

9. What is the great invitation that Jesus offers to the weary? (Matthew 11:28-30)

10. Why did Jesus reprove Simon, the Pharisee, and what parable did he use in his reproof? (Luke 7:37-50)

11. Whom did Jesus heal of evil spirits and infirmities? (Luke 8:2-3)

12. What was the teaching of Jesus regarding his mother and brothers? (Luke 8:19-21)

13. Name the four kinds of soil mentioned in the Parable of the Sower and tell what type of hearer each symbolizes. (Matthew 13:3-23)

14. Write a synopsis of each of the following: "The Parable of the Tares," "The Parable of the Mustard Seed," "The Parable of the Leaven," and "The Hidden Treasure." (Matthew 13:24-46.)

Memorize:

"Come unto me, all ye that labor and are heavy laden, and I will give you rest. Take my yoke upon you, and learn of me; for I am meek and lowly in heart: and ye shall find rest unto your souls. For my yoke is easy, and my burden is light." Matthew 11:28-30.

"Lord, to whom shall we go? Thou hast the words of eternal life." John 6:68.

Quotations for careful study:

"Art thou He that should come, or look we for another?" Luke 7:19.

Christ's tribute to John the Baptist: "Among those that are born of women there hath not risen a greater than John the Baptist." Matthew 11:11.

Jesus proclaims John the Baptist as His forerunner: "This is He of whom it is written, 'Behold I send my messenger before thy face, which shall prepare thy way before thee.'" Luke 7:27.

. . . .

Explain the terms: *blasphemy, parable, tare, "sackcloth and ashes."*

Lesson VII

The Great Galilean Ministry of Christ (continued)

*54. The stilling of a storm on the Sea of Galilee
Matthew 8:18-27. Mark 4:35-41. Luke 8:22-25.**

55. The healing of the demoniac at Gergesa; devils enter swine
Matthew 8:28-34. Mark 5:1-21. Luke 8:26-40.**

56. The feast of Matthew and the discourses on fasting
Matthew 9:10-17. Mark 2:15-22. Luke 5:29-39.**

57. The raising of the daughter of Jairus and the curing of a woman
Matthew 9:18-26. Mark 5:22-43. Luke 8:41-56.**

58. The healing of two blind men and one dumb person
Matthew 9:27-34.**

59. The rejection at Nazareth (again?)
Matthew 13:53-58.** Mark 6:1-6.

60. The third tour of Galilee and the sending out of the Twelve
Matthew 9:35-11:1.** Mark 6:6-13. Luke 9:1-6.**

61. The fear of Herod that Jesus is John the Baptist risen from the dead
Matthew 14:1-12.** Mark 6:14-29. Luke 9:7-9.**

62. The report of the Twelve and the retirement with Jesus to a desert place
Matthew 14:13. Mark 6:30-32. Luke 9:10-11.** John 6:1.

* The starred (*) events are to be stressed.
** The basic references for this course are double-starred. Pupils should read all references, individually or cooperatively.

*63. The feeding of the five thousand
   Matthew 14:13-21. Mark 6:32-44. Luke 9:12-17.**
   John 6:1-14.

64. The walk on the sea
   Matthew 14:22-36. Mark 6:45-56. John 6:15-21.**

*65. The discourse on the Bread of Life; some disciples turn back and follow Him no more. He speaks to the twelve
   John 6:22-7:1**

Questions—Lesson VII.

The Discourse on the Bread of Life. (John 6:22-7:1)

1. Why did the people follow Jesus into Capernaum? (26) What did He exhort them to do? (27) What did He say the work of God is? (29) What did they ask of Him, and what was their reason? (30)
2. What is the Bread from heaven, the Bread of God, the Bread of Life? (32, 33, 35) Why did Jesus come down from heaven? (38) What is the will of God? (40)
3. How does one come to Christ? (44) How is He drawn? (45)
4. Had Jesus yet sacrificed His flesh or body? (51) When did He do so?
5. Were all of His disciples true believers? (64) Explain verse 66.
6. What did Peter say when Jesus asked the twelve if they would also go away? (68)

Memorize:

"Lord, to whom shall we go? Thou hast the words of eternal life." John 6:68.

"And this is the will of him that sent me, that every one which seeth the Son, and believeth on him, may have everlasting life: and I will raise him up at the last day." John 6:40.

Quotations for careful study:

"A prophet is not without honor, save in his own country, and in his own house." Matthew 13:57.

"I am the bread of life." John 6:35.

"It is I; be not afraid." John 6:20.

. . . .

Explain the following terms: *Testament* and *straightway*.

Lesson VIII

The Great Galilean Ministry of Christ (continued)

66. The answer to the Pharisees' criticism of the disciples
    Matthew 15:1-20.** Mark 7:1-23.

67. The healing of the Syrophoenician woman's daughter
    Matthew 15:21-28.** Mark 7:24-30.

68. The healing of many in Decapolis, including the deaf stammerer
    Matthew 15:29-31. Mark 7:31-37.**

69. The feeding of the four thousand
    Matthew 15:32-38. Mark 8:1-9.**

70. The refusing to give the Pharisees a sign at Dalmanutha
    Matthew 15:39-16:4. Mark 8:10-12.**

71. The departure and warning to his disciples against the leaven of the Pharisees
    Matthew 16:5-12. Mark 8:13-21.**

72. The healing of a blind man who saw men as trees walking
    Mark 8:22-26.**

73. The questioning of His disciples; the great Confession by Peter
    Matthew 16:13-20. Mark 8:27-30. Luke 9:18-20.

74. The foretelling of His death and resurrection
    Matthew 16:21-28. Mark 8:31-9:1. Luke 9:21-27.

*75. The transfiguration
    Matthew 17:1-13. Mark 9:2-13. Luke 9:28-36.

76. The healing of the demoniac boy after the disciples failed.
    Matthew 17:14-21. Mark 9:14-29. Luke 9:37-43.

77. The prediction of His Passion
    Matthew 17:22-23. Mark 9:30-32. Luke 9:43-45.

78. The paying of tribute money
    Matthew 17:24-27.**

---

* The starred (*) events are to be stressed.
** The basic references for this course are double-starred. Pupils should read all references, individually or cooperatively.

79. The answering of the disciples' question concerning greatness
     Matthew 18:1-14. Mark 9:33-50. Luke 9:46-50.

*80. The teaching concerning forgiveness; the parable of the wicked servant
     Matthew 18:15-35.**

81. His rejection of his brothers' proposal that He go to Judea to manifest His greatness
     John 7:2-9.

82. The making of a private journey to Jerusalem
     (SIC) Luke 9:51-56. John 7:10.

83. The teaching concerning the necessity of sacrificing all for His sake
     (SIC) Luke 9:57-62.

Questions—Lesson VIII.

The Transfiguration of Christ (Luke 9:28-36; Matthew 17:1-13)

1. Why did Christ go into the mountain, and whom did He take with Him? (28)

2. Describe the change that took place in His appearance as He prayed. (29; Matthew 17:2) What two men appeared and talked with Him, and of what did they speak? (30, 31)

3. What did the voice that came out of the cloud say? 34, 45)

His teaching Concerning Forgiveness; Parable of the Wicked Servant. (Matthew 18:15-35)

4. What question concerning forgiving did Peter ask, and what was Christ's answer? (21, 22)

5. What parable did Christ then give concerning forgiving? (23-34)

6. What application did He make of it? (35)

Memorize:
    "Not that which goeth into the mouth defileth a man; but that which cometh out of the mouth, this defileth a man." Matthew 15:11.

Quotations for careful study:
"Thou art the Christ, the son of the living God." Matthew 16:16.

"Master, it is good for us to be here." Mark 9:5.

What one must do in order to follow Christ: "If any man come after me, let him deny himself, and take up his cross daily, and follow me." Luke 9:23.

. . . .

Locate Caesarea, Philippi, and Mt. Herman.

Explain the following terms: *transfiguration, talent,* and *parable.*

Identify Moses and Elijah.

Lesson IX

The Great Galilean Ministry of Christ (continued)

84. The teaching in the Temple at Feast of Tabernacles
   John 7:11-52.**

85. The convicting of the accusers of the adulteress
   John 7:53-8:11.**

86. The proclaiming Himself the Light, the Messiah, and answering the Jews, and escaping when they attempt to stone Him
   John 8:12-59.**

87. The healing of a man born blind
   John 9:1-41.**

*88. The giving of the parable of the Good Shepherd
   John 10:1-21.**

Questions—Lesson IX.

The Parable of the Good Shepherd and Its Explanations (John 10:1-21)

1. Relate the parable. (1-5) Did the Pharisees understand it? (6)

2. Jesus explains that He is the door. (7-10) Summarize His explanation.

---

* The starred (*) events are to be stressed.
** The basic references for this course are double-starred. Pupils should read all references, individually or cooperatively.

3. Explain His meaning in verse 16.

4. He explains that He is the Good Shepherd. (11-17) Give His explanation.

5. Did Jesus willingly sacrifice His life? (17-18)

6. What effect did Jesus' words have upon the Jews? (19-21)

Memorize:
"And ye shall know the truth, and the truth shall make you free." John 8:32.

Quotations for careful study:
"I am the Light of the world." John 8:12.
"I am the good shepherd, and know my sheep, and am known of mine." John 10:14.

. . . .

Explain *Messiah* and *Feast of the Tabernacle.*

Lesson X

V. *The Perean Ministry of Christ*

*89. The sending out of the seventy; their returning, and reporting
    Luke 10:1-24.**

*90. The parable of the Good Samaritan
    Luke 10:25-37.**

91. The visiting in the home of Martha and Mary in Bethany
    Luke 10:38-42.**

92. The teaching concerning prayer in answer to the disciples' request
    Luke 11:1-13.**

93. The answering of the attacks of the Pharisees
    Luke 11:14-54.**

94. The teaching concerning hypocrisy, blasphemy, covetousness, worldly anxiety, and preparedness
    Luke 12:1-49.**

95. The predictions and exhortations
    Luke 12:50-59.**

96. The teaching on repentance in answer to a report
    Luke 13:1-5.**

97. The parable of the barren fig tree
    Luke 13:6-9.**

98. The healing of the cripple on the Sabbath, and the answering of criticism of rulers
    Luke 13:10-17.**

99. The parables of the mustard seed and the leaven
    Luke 13:18-21.**

Questions—Lesson X.

The Sending of the Seventy and Their Return (Luke 10:1-24)

1. Where did Jesus send the seventy? (1) What general directions did He give them for their journey? (4) What directions concerning any house where they would stay? (5-7) Concerning any city they should visit? (8-12) What cities did he mention that especially deserved condemnation and why? (13-15)

2. What was the relation of the seventy to Christ and to God? (16)

3. What was their report when they returned from their mission? (17)

4. What power did Christ give them? (19) For what should they rejoice? (20)

5. For what did Christ thank the Father? (21)

6. How did He describe His relation to God? (22)

7. Why were the disciples who lived then especially blessed? (23, 24)

Memorize:

"Take heed, and beware of covetousness: for a man's life consisteth not in the abundance of the things which he possesseth." Luke 12:15.

Quotations for careful study:

"The life is more than meat, and the body is more than raiment." Luke 12:23.

. . . .

Locate Bethany and Perea.

Explain the term, *covet.*

---

* The starred (*) events are to be stressed.
** The basic references for this course are double-starred. Pupils should read all references, individually or cooperatively.

Lesson XI

The Perean Ministry of Christ (continued)

100. The discourses at the Feast of Dedication; escaping, retiring beyond Jordan
John 10:22-42.**

101. The teaching and journeying back toward Jerusalem; strait gate
Luke 13:22-35.**

102. The dining with a Pharisee
Luke 14:1-24.**

103. The requirements for discipleship
Luke 14:25-35.**

104. The three parables justifying His receiving publicans and sinners
Luke 15:1-32.**

105. The parable of the unjust steward
Luke 16:1-13.**

106. The parable of the Rich Man and Lazarus told to the covetous Pharisees
Luke 16:14-31.**

107. The teaching concerning faith, forgiveness, and service
Luke 17:1-10.**

108. The raising of Lazarus from the dead at Bethany
John 11:1-44.**

109. The results: Many believe, rulers hold council, Caiaphas prophesies, Jesus retires to Ephraim
John 11:45-54.**

Questions—Lesson XI.

Teachings Concerning Faith, Forgiveness, Service (Luke 17:1-10)

1. What warning did Jesus address to the disciples concerning giving offenses? (1, 2) Concerning forgiving offenses? (3, 4)

2. What request did the apostles then make of Him? (5) How did He reply? (6) Do you thnk He meant common faith or miraculous faith?

3. What lesson did Jesus teach through the story of the servant in verses 7-9? (10)

Memorize:

Jesus, the promise of a new life: "I am the resurrection, and the life: he that believeth in me, though he were dead, yet shall he live." John 11:25.

. . . .

Locate Ephraim.

Explain the following terms: *counsel, council, husks,* and *Feast of Dedication.*

Identify Lazarus (beggar) and Lazarus (of Bethany).

Explain *blasphemy.*

Lesson XII

The Perean Ministry of Christ (continued)

110. The journey to Jerusalem for Passover; healing ten lepers on the way; explaining the coming of the Kingdom
    Luke 17:11-37.**

111. The parable of the importunate widow
    Luke 18:1-8.**

*112. The parable of the Pharisee and the publican
    Luke 18:9-14.**

113. The answers to the Pharisees concerning divorce
    Matthew 19:1-12.** Mark 10:2-12.

114. The blessing of little children, and rebuking of disciples
    Matthew 19:13-15 Mark 10:13-16. Luke 18:15-17.**

115. The answers to the rich young ruler
    Matthew 19:16-30. Mark 10:17-31. Luke 18:18-30.**

116. The parable of the laborers in the vineyard
    Matthew 20:1-16.**

117. The prediction, again, of His death and Resurrection
    Matthew 20:17-19. Mark 10:32-34. Luke 18:31-34.**

118. The rebuking of the ambition of James and John
    Matthew 20:20-28.** Mark 10:35-45.

---

* The starred (*) events are to be stressed.
** The basic references for this course are double-starred. Pupils should read all references, individually or cooperatively.

119. The healing of Bartimeus and his companion, both blind
     Matthew 20:29-34. Mark 10:46-52. Luke 18:35-43.**

120. The visit to Zaccheus, the publican, at Jericho
     Luke 19:1-10.**

121. The parable of the pounds
     Luke 19:11-28.**

Questions—Lesson XII.

1. Which of the ten lepers came back to thank Jesus for healing him? (Luke 17:16)

2. Why did the disciples have difficulty in understanding what Jesus said about coming events in his life? (Luke 17:20-37)

3. What is the meaning of the Parable of the Importunate Woman? (Luke 18:1-8)

4. What lesson is taught in the Parable of the Pharisee and the Publican? (Luke 18:9-14)

5. How did Jesus answer the questions of the Pharisees concerning divorce? (Matthew 19:1-12)

6. a. Why did Jesus rebuke his disciples? (Mark 10:13-14)
   b. Explain Mark 10:15.
   c. What are some of the qualities which belonged to you as a child that you must keep as you grow, if you are to be a part of Christ's Kingdom?

7. a. Why did the rich young ruler go away sorrowful? (Luke 18:18-30)
   b. Is it possible for the rich to go to Heaven? (Mark 10:24-27)
   c. How may riches be a real blessing?

8. What is the meaning of the Parable of the Laborers in the Vineyard? (Matthew 20:1-16)

9. What did Jesus foretell as he and his disciples journeyed toward Jerusalem? (Luke 18:31-34)

10. Jesus rebuked James and John because of what misunderstanding? (Matthew 20:20-28)

11. What is Jesus' measure of greatness? (Matthew 20:26-28)

12. a. Whom did Jesus heal by the way near Jericho? (Mark 10:46)

b. Relate the circumstances which led to the healing. (Mark 10:45-52)

13. a. Why did the Pharisees murmur when Jesus went into the house of Zacchaeus? (Luke 19:7)

   b. What were the evidences of Zacchaeus' conversion? (Luke 19:8-10)

14. Explain the meaning of the Parable of the Pounds. (Luke 19:11-28)

Memorize:

Christ's measure of greatness:

"But whosoever will be great among you, let him be your minister; And whosoever will be chief among you, let him be your servant: Even as the Son of man came not to be ministered unto, but to minister, and to give his life a ransom for many." Matthew 20:26-28.

Quotations for careful study:

"God be merciful to me a sinner." Luke 18:13.

"Suffer little children, and forbid them not, to come unto me; for of such is the kingdom of heaven." Matthew 19:14.

. . . .

Locate Jericho.

Explain the following terms: *importunate, millstone, offend,* and *pounds.*

Identify Zaccheus and Bartimeus.

Lesson XIII

VI. The Last Week of Christ's Earthly Life

122. The arrival in Bethany, the annointing by Mary, the answering of Judas, the multitudes
Matthew 26:6-13. Mark 14:3-9. John 11:55-12:11.**

Sunday

*123. The triumphal entry into Jerusalem
Matthew 21:1-11. Mark 11:1-11. Luke 19:29-44.**
John 12:12-19.**

---

* The starred (*) events are to be stressed.
** The basic references for this course are double-starred. Pupils should read all references, individually or cooperatively.

Monday

124. The cursing of the barren fig tree
     Matthew 21:17-19.   Mark 11:12-14.**

125. The cleansing of the Temple
     Matthew 21:12-17.   Mark 11:15-19.   Luke 19:45-48.**

Tuesday

126. The finding of the withered fig tree and the teaching of the lesson on faith
     Matthew 21:20-22.   Mark 11:20-26.**   Luke 21:37-38.

127. The answer to the Sanhedrin who had challenged His authority
     Matthew 21:23-27.   Mark 11:27-33.   Luke 20:1-8.**

128. The continuation of His answer: the parable of the two sons, the parable of the wicked husbandman, the marriage of the king's son
     Matthew 21:28-22:14.**   Mark 12:1-12.   Luke 20:9-19.

*129. The answer to the Pharisees and Herodians about paying tribute
     Matthew 22:15-22.   Mark 12:13-17.   Luke 20:20-26.**

*130. The answer to the Sadducees concerning the resurrection
     Matthew 22:23-33.   Mark 12:18-27.   Luke 20:27-39.**

*131. The answer to the lawyer concerning the great commandment
     Matthew 22:34-40.   Mark 12:28-34.

132. The asking of a question the Pharisees could not answer
     Matthew 22:41-46.   Mark 12:35-37.   Luke 20:41-44.**

133. The pronouncing of woes against the scribes and Pharisees
     Matthew 23:1-36.**   Mark 12:38-40.   Luke 20:45-47.

134. The lamentation over Jerusalem
     Matthew 23:37-39.**

Questions—Lesson XIII.

The Triumphal Entry into Jerusalem (Luke 19:29-44; John 12:12-19)

1. Describe the triumphal entry.

2. What prophecy was fullfilled on this occasion? (John 12:14-15)

3. What did the Pharisees say among themselves? (John 12:19)

4. What did some of the Pharisees say to Jesus? (Luke 19:39)

5. What did He reply? (40)

Christ's Enemies Fail in Their Efforts to Entangle Him (Matthew 22:15-46; Luke 20:20-44)

6. What did the chief priest and scribes resort to in their efforts to obtain a cause for the arrest of Christ? (Luke 20:20)

7. What was their first question with this object in view? (22) How did Christ answer it? (23-25) What was the effect of His answer? (26)

8. What question did the Sadducees then submit? (27-33) His answer? (34, 35)

9. With what query did the Pharisee lawyer make his attempt? (Matthew 22:34-36) Give Christ's answer. (37-40)

10. What question did Jesus then ask the Pharisees? (41, 42) Their answer? (42) What did he next ask and what was the result? (43-46)

Memorize:

The Great Commandment: "Thou shalt love the Lord thy God with all thy heart, and with all thy soul, and with all thy mind. This is the first and great commandment. And the second is like unto it, Thou shalt love they neighbor as thyself. On these two commandments hang all the law and the prophets." Matthew 22:37-40.

Quotations for careful study:

"Render unto Caesar the things which are Caesar's; and unto God the things that are God's." Matthew 22:21.

. . . .

Explain the following terms: *Sanhedrin* and *Sadducees.*

Lesson XIV

The Last Week of Christ's Earthly Life (continued)

135. The observance of offerings and commendation of widow's mite
  Mark 12:41-44. Luke 21:1-4.**

*136. The desire of the Greeks to see Him; His glorification is confirmed
  John 12:20-50.**

*137. The prediction of the destruction of Jerusalem and His second coming
  Matthew 24:1-51. Mark 13:1-37. Luke 21:5-36.**

138. The parable of the ten virgins
  Matthew 25:1-13.**

139. The parable of the talents
  Matthew 25:14-30.**

140. The teaching concerning the final judgment
  Matthew 25:31-46.**

141. The prediction of His betrayal and crucifixion
  Matthew 26:1-2.**

142. The planning of His betrayal and death by Judas and rulers
  Matthew 26:3-5, 14-16. Mark 14:1-11. Luke 22:1-6.**

Thursday

143. The instructions to the disciples who prepare for the Passover
  Matthew 26:17-19. Mark 14:12-16. Luke 22:7-13.**

*144. The teaching on greatness when the disciples strive for places of honor and preferment
  Luke 22:24-30.**

*145. The washing of the disciples' feet; lesson in humility and service
  John 13:1-20.

Questions—Lesson XIV.

Concerning the Glorification of Christ (John 12:23-50)

1. What did Jesus tell Andrew and Philip concerning the time of His glorification? (23)

2. What illustration from nature did He use to explain what was about to take place? (24) Why was His soul troubled? (27)

3. What did He ask of the Father, and what was the response? (28) What did the people say about this manifestation? (29) For what did Jesus tell them it came? (30)

4. What did Jesus signify when He said, "If I be lifted up?" (32, 33) What was the people's reply to His statement about being lifted up? (34) Did they yet understand the nature of Christ's kingdom? Did they believe on Him? Had they had sufficient evidence to produce faith? (37) Did any of the chief rulers believe on Him and confess Him? Why? (42, 43)

5. How does Christ here describe His unity with God? (44, 45, 49)

6. For what reason did He come to earth? (47) How and when will those who reject Him be judged? (48)

Concerning the Coming of Christ. (Luke 21:20-36)

7. Name some of the signs that Christ said would indicate His coming. (20-27) What parable did He give to illustrate His meaning? (29-31)

8. Name some of His exhortations. (28, 34, 36)

Concerning the Final Judgment (Matthew 25:31-46)

9. Summarize Christ's description of the final judgment.

10. Note that this was the conclusion of His last public discourse.

Lessons on Humility and Service (Luke 22:24-30; John 13:1-20)

11. Summarize what Jesus said to His disciples who contended for greatness in His kingdom. (Luke 22:26)

12. What lesson did He teach by example when He washed their feet? (John 13:12-16)

Memorize:

How enduring is Christ's word?

"Heaven and earth shall pass away: but my words shall not pass away." Luke 21:33.

How can we minister to Christ?

"Inasmuch as ye have done it unto one of the least of these my brethren, ye have done it unto me." Matthew 25:40.

Quotations for careful study:

"Well done, good and faithful servant; thou hast been faithful over a few things: enter thou into the joy of the Lord." Matthew 25:23.

"For I was an hungered, and ye gave me meat: I was thirsty and ye gave me drink: I was a stranger and ye took me in:

"Naked and ye clothed me: I was sick, and ye visited me: I was in prison and ye came unto me." Matthew 25:35, 36.

Lesson XV

The Last Week of Christ's Earthly Life (continued)

146. The foretelling of Judas's betrayal and Peter's denial
   Matthew 26:20-25.   Mark 14:18-21.   Luke 22:21-23.
   Matthew 26:30-38.   Mark 14:26-31.   Luke 22:31-38.
   John 13:21-38.**

*147. The institution of the Lord's Supper
   Matthew 26:26-29.   Mark 14:22-25.**   Luke 22:17-20.

*148. The farewell discourse to His disciples
   John 14 to 16.**

*149. The prayer for glorification and for His present and future disciples
   John 17:1-26.**

150. The agony in Gethsemane
   Matthew 26:36-46.   Mark 14:32-42.   Luke 22:39-46.**
   John 18:1.

Friday

*151. The betrayal, arrest, and desertion by the disciples
   Matthew 26:47-56.   Mark 14:43-52.   Luke 22:47-54.**
   John 18:2-11.

Questions—Lesson XV.

The Institution of the Lord's Supper   (Matthew 26:26-29; Mark 14:22-25)

1. Where were Jesus and the disciples and what had they been doing when He instituted the Lord's Supper?

2. Compare Matthew's and Mark's accounts of the instituting of the Supper.

Christ's Farewell Discourse to His Disciples and His Prayer Following

3. Relate at least one thing that Christ taught in His farewell sermon concerning each of the following topics: (1) faith, (2) the Way, (3) prayer, (4) love, (5) the Comforter. (John, Chapters 14, 15, 16)

4. For what and whom did He pray following this discourse? (John 17:1-26)

Christ's Betrayal and Arrest

5. Tell the story of His betrayal and arrest. (Luke 22:47-54)

Memorize:

The importance of watching and praying:

"Watch ye and pray, lest ye enter into temptation. The spirit truly is ready, but the flesh is weak." Mark 14:38.

Christ's consolation to believers:

"Let not your heart be troubled: ye believe in God, believe also in me. In my Father's house are many mansions: If it were not so, I would have told you. I go to prepare a place for you. And if I go and prepare a place for you, I will come again, and receive you unto myself; that where I am, there ye may be also." John 14:1-3.

Quotations for careful study:

"This do in remembrance of me." Luke 22:19.

"Herein is my Father glorified, that ye bear much fruit: so shall ye be my disciples." John 15:8

. . . .

Locate Gethsemane and Mount of Olives.

Explain the following terms: *betray, ordinance,* and *Comforter.*

Lesson XVI

The Last Week of Christ's Earthly Life (continued)

152. The appearing of Christ before Annas, who sends Him to Caiaphas

John 18:12-14,** 19-24.

---

* The starred (*) events are to be stressed.

** The basic references for this course are double-starred. Pupils should read all references, individually or cooperatively.

153. The condemnation by Caiaphas and members of the Sanhedrin
     Matthew 26:57-68.**   Mark 14:55-56.   Luke 22:54, 63-65.

154. The denial by Peter three times
     Matthew 26:69-75.   Mark 14:66-72.   Luke 22:54-62.
     John 18:15-18, 25-27.**

155. Carried before Sanhedrin in session; led to Pilate
     Matthew 27:1-2.   Mark 15:1.   Luke 22:66** 23:1.

156. The appearing before Pilate who finds no fault in Him
     Matthew 27:11-14.   Mark 15:2-5.   Luke 23:2-7
     John 18:28-38.**

157. The appearing before Herod, where Christ remains silent and is sent back to Pilate
     Luke 23:8-12.**

158. The sentence reluctantly given by Pilate when the people demand it
     Matthew 27:15-26.   Mark 15:6-15.   Luke 23:13-25.**
     John 18:39-19:16.

159. The repentance of Judas, who returns the silver and hangs himself
     Matthew 27:3-10.**

160. The mocking by the soldiers who lead Him away to be crucified
     Matthew 27:27-32.**   Mark 15:16-23.**   Luke 23:26-33.

161. The crucifixion and reviling
     Matthew 27:33-44.**   Mark 15:24-32.**   Luke 23:33-43.
     John 19:17-27.

162. The utterance of three sayings during first three hours
     Luke 23:34,43.**   John 19:26.**

163. The darkness over the earth the next three hours
     Matthew 27:45-49.   Mark 15:33.   Luke 23:44-45.**

164. The utterance of four more sayings, and death
     Mark 15:34.**   Luke 23:46.**   John 19:28-30.**

165. The death of Christ attended by supernatural events
     Matthew 27:50-56.**   Mark 15:35-41.   Luke 23:45.
     John 19:31-42.

166. His condition: dead, no bones broken, side pierced
     John 19:31-37.**

167. The burial
>   Matthew 27:57-60.   Mark 15:42-47.   Luke 23:50-56.
>   John 19:38-42.**

Saturday

168. The guarding of the sepulcher
>   Matthew 27:62-66.**

Questions—Lesson XVI.

Christ's Trial, Crucifixion, and Burial.

1. Name the three stages of the Jewish trial, and tell briefly what was done at each. (John 18:12-14; Luke 22:54, 63-23:1; John 18:19-24)

2. Tell about Peter's denial. (Luke 22:54-62; John 18:15-18; 25-27)

3. Name the three stages of the Roman trial, and tell briefly what happened at each. (Luke 23:2-25)

4. What became of Judas, and why? What became of the silver for which he sold Jesus? (Matthew 27:3-10)

5. How was Jesus treated during the interval between His sentence and His crucifixion? (Matthew 27:27-34)

6. What became of the garments of Jesus? (Matthew 27:35)

7. What inscription was placed over His head as He hanged on the cross? (37)

8. Who were crucified with Jesus? (38)

9. What did the people who passed by do and say while He was on the cross? (39-40)

10. What did the chief priests and scribes say? (41-43)

11. Contrast the attitude of the two thieves toward Christ. (Luke 23:39-42) What promise did Jesus make to one of them? (43)

12. Give Christ's three sayings during the first three hours on the cross. (Luke 23:34, 43; John 19:26, 27)

13. What happened during the next three hours? (Luke 23:44)

14. Give his last four recorded sayings on the cross. (Mark 15:34; Luke 23:46; John 19:28-30)

---

* The starred (*) events are to be stressed.
** The basic references for this course are double-starred. Pupils should read all references, individually or cooperatively.

15. Name three supernatural events that attended the death of Christ. (Matthew 27:50-52) (Note the statement that the bodies of the saints were resurrected after Christ's resurrection. Christ Himself was the "First-born from the dead;" (Colossians 1:18)

16. What effect did these events have upon the centurion and those watching with him, and what did they say? (Matthew 27:54)

17. Why were the legs of Jesus not broken as was customary under like circumstances? (John 19:31-33, 36) What other prophecy did the soldiers fulfill? (34-37)

18. Tell about the burial of Jesus. (John 19:38-42)

19. Why did the Jews seal the tomb of Christ and set a watch over it? (Matthew 27:62-66)

Memorize:

The seven recorded sayings of Jesus on the cross:

"Father, forgive them; for they know not what they do." Luke 23:34.

"Verily I say unto thee, Today shalt thou be with me in Paradise." Luke 23:43.

"Woman, behold thy son!" . . . "Behold thy mother!" John 19:26, 27.

"My God, my God, why hast thou forsaken me?" Mark 15:34.

"I thirst." John 19:28.

"It is finished." John 19:30.

"Father, into thy hands I commend my spirit." Luke 23:46.

Quotations for careful study:

"They parted my garments among them, and upon my vesture did they cast lots." Matthew 27:35.

"Certainly this was a righteous man. Luke 23:47.

. . . .

Locate Mount of Olives and Golgotha.

Define the following terms: *crucify, buffet, malefactor,* and *passion.*

Identify Annas, Caiaphas, Joseph of Arimathea, Herod, Pilate, Barabbas, and Simon of Cyrene.

Lesson XVII

VII. The Resurrection, Appearances After His Resurrection, and the Ascension

Sunday

169. The women find the empty tomb, talk with angel, tell the eleven
     Matthew 28:1-8.   Mark 16:1-8.   Luke 24:1-12.**
     John 20:1-10.

170. The appearance of Jesus to Mary Magdalene, and the sending of the message to the disciples
     Mark 16:9-11.   John 20:11-18.**

171. The appearance to the other women and the sending of the message
     Matthew 28:8-10.**

172. The guards are bribed to give false report about His escape
     Matthew 28:11-15.**

173. The appearance of Christ to the two disciples on the way to Emmaus
     Mark 16:12-13.   Luke 24:13-32.**

174. The report of the two disciples to the eleven of His appearances to them and to Peter
     Luke 24:33-35.**

175. The appearance to the ten in Jerusalem; Thomas absent, doubts
     Mark 16:14.   Luke 24:36-43.**   John 20:24-25.**

176. The appearance one week later to all the eleven
     John 20:26-31.**

177. The appearance to the seven at the Sea of Galilee; the restoration of Peter
     John 21:1-25.**

*178. The appearance to the apostles and the giving of the Great Commission
     Matthew 28:16-20.**   Mark 16:15-18.   Luke 24:46-47.

179. The promising of the Holy Spirit
     Luke 24:49

---

* The starred (*) events are to be stressed.
** The basic references for this course are double-starred. Pupils should read all references, individually or cooperatively.

180. The ascension in the presence of the apostles
Mark 16:19. Luke 24:50-51.

Note—In addition to the above recorded appearances by the writers of the Gospel, Paul mentions (I Corinthians 15:5-8) that Christ appeared also:

(1)   To above five hundred brethren at once (believed by authorities to be identified with the appearance of 178 above) ;

(2)   To James;

(3)   To Paul on his way to Damascus.

Questions—Lesson XVII.

Christ's Resurrection, Appearances, and Ascension

1. Who went to Christ's tomb? When and why? What did they find? Who spoke to them? To whom did they report? Were they believed? (Luke 24:1-12)

2. How many appearances did Jesus make to women? What were the messages He gave them, and to whom were the messages to be delivered? (John 20:11-18; Matthew 28:8-10)

3. What did some of the guards do about the empty tomb? What did the chief priests do? (Matthew 28:11-15)

4. About what were the two disciples to whom Jesus appeared on the way to Emmaus troubled? What was Jesus's criticism, and how did He strengthen their faith and hope? When and how did He reveal Himself to them? When they reported this appearance to the eleven, what other appearance did they mention? (Luke 24:13-35)

5. What happened while the two were relating their story? What was the effect, and what did Jesus do? How did He prove to them His identity? (Luke 24:36-43) Which of the apostles was absent on this occasion? Did he believe their report? What did he say about it? (John 20:24, 25) Was he ever convinced? How? (26-28) What did Jesus then say to him? (29)

6. How were the disciples at the Sea of Galilee convinced that it was Christ who appeared to them? Tell about the recall of Peter here. What prediction was made concerning Peter? Did Jesus say that John would not die? (John 21:1-25)

7. Who were with the apostles in Galilee where Jesus had promised to meet them? (I Corinthians 15:6) (That

makes it easier to understand why there were present some who doubted.) What was the great event of this meeting? (Mark 16:16-20)

8. What promise did Jesus make to the apostles when He appeared to them the last time in Jerusalem? (Luke 24:44-49)

9. What was Jesus's last act before His ascension? (Luke 24:50-51)

Memorize:

The purpose of the Gospel:

"But these are written, that ye may believe that Jesus is the Christ, the Son of God; and that believing ye might have life through his name."   John 20:31.

Quotations for careful study:

"Did not our heart burn within us, while He talked with us by the way, and while He opened to us the Scriptures?" Luke 24:32.

"He is not here, but is risen."   Luke 24:6.

. . . .

Locate Emmaus.

Identify Mary Magdalene, Joanna, Mary (mother of James), Salome, and Cleopas.

PART TWO
ACTS OF THE APOSTLES

INTRODUCTION

The Acts of the Apostles takes up the history of Christianity at the ascension of Christ and continues it through the arrival of Paul at Rome after his appeal to Caesar. It was written by Luke, in considerable part from his own observation of the facts narrated.

The Acts of the Apostles is divided into two parts. The first part, chapters one to twelve, is an account of the growth of the Church in Jerusalem and from Jerusalem as a center. The central figure is Simon Peter who had been an ardently loyal as well as a cowardly follower of Jesus during His three years of earthly ministry. However, Peter was no longer that mixture of strange contradictions but was the "rock" which Jesus prophesied he would become. On the Day of Pentecost, strengthened by the baptism of the Holy Spirit, he stood immovable before the great throng assembled from the four corners of the earth and courageously declared that the crucified Christ was the Messiah of whom the prophets had spoken since the world began. He became a great leader in the Jerusalem Church, preaching and healing. Great multitudes even sought the healing power of his shadow. For the sake of Christ and His Church, he suffered persecution and imprisonment, but in spite of this opposition made triumphant progress. After the vision on the housetop at Joppa, Peter worked with Paul in taking the Gospel to the Gentiles. It is possible that his evangelistic tours took him as far east as Babylon (I Peter 5:13).

The second part of The Acts of the Apostles, chapters thirteen to twenty-eight, relates the history of the extension of the Church through the empire. Antioch became the great missionary center and the Apostle Paul the new leader, the narrative dealing largely with his labors.

Next to the Lord Jesus, Christianity owes more to the Apostle Paul than to any other person. He was a Roman citizen by birth and was influenced by the cosmopolitan atmosphere of his native city, Tarsus. Taught by Gamaliel, the greatest Jewish Rabbi of the day, Paul excelled in the knowledge of the law. His mastery of the scriptures is shown by his later writings. He was exceedingly zealous for the Jewish faith, and after his conversion he exalted the cause of Christ with the same intense earnestness. He carried the gospel out into distant places, secured for it the first wide hearing among the Gentiles, and established churches in many important centers. He has interpreted the life and teachings of Christ and left inspired writings that make up a large part of our New Testament. Paul gave to the world the greatest example of all times of energy, courage, self-sacrifice, and devoted loyalty to Christ.

In addition to Peter and Paul, the other chief witnesses mentioned in Acts are Philip, Stephen, John Mark, and Barnabas.

Lesson XVIII

The Early Church (A.D.   30-36)

I. The Church in Jerusalem (Read Acts 1:1 to 8:2.)

    A. The Foundation of the Church.

        1. Upon what truth was the Lord's Church built? Matthew 16:13-19; I Corinthians 3:11.

        2. How was the Church purchased?   Acts 20:28.

        3. Who is the chief cornerstone of the Church?   Ephesians 2:20.

        4. Who is the head of the Church?   Ephesians 5:23; Colossians 1:18.

        5. What did Jesus commission His followers to do? Matthew 28:18-20.

        6. Before carrying out this Great Commission, what did Jesus instruct His disciples to do?   Act 1:4-8; Luke 24:49.

        7. Read of the activities of the apostles from the ascension until they received the promise of the Father on the day of Pentecost. Acts 1:9-26.

    B. The Establishment of the Church.

        1. Where were the apostles when the Holy Ghost came upon them and they received power? Acts 2:1-4.

        2. What great occasion was being celebrated? Acts 2:1 (Pentecost — meaning "fiftieth" — an annual feast day of the Jews. At the beginning of the harvest, the offering of First Fruits was made. Fifty days thereafter was Pentecost. Leviticus 23:9-16. The Pentecost mentioned in Acts 2:1

was the first Pentecost after Christ, our "First Fruits," came from the grave. I Corinthians 15:20.)

3. Study the first complete Gospel sermon. Acts 2:14-40.

4. What was the result of Peter's sermon? Acts 2:37-41.

C. Characteristics of the Church.

1. What characterized these first members of the Church? Acts 2:42.

2. Why the necessity for the community of goods? Acts 2:44, 45.

3. How did the membership of the Church increase? Acts 2:47.

4. What caused the Church to come together in prayer, united in "one heart and of one soul" as recorded in Acts 4:23-37; Acts 3:1-26; 4:1-22.

5. Tell the story of Ananias and Sapphira. Why this strict discipline in the early Church? Acts 5:1-16.

6. Read of Peter's second imprisonment. What advice did Gamaliel give the court? Acts 5:17-40.

7. What was the reaction of the apostles to the beating and to the command of the Sanhedrin? Acts 5:41, 42.

8. Tell of the selection of the first deacons. Acts 6:1-6.

9. Read the entire account of the first Christian Martyr. Acts 6:5 to 8:2.

Memorize:

What did Peter and the other apostles say when reprimanded by the high priest for preaching Christ?

"We ought to obey God rather than man." Acts 5:29.

Quotations for careful study:

"And when the day of Pentecost was fully come, they were all with one accord in one place." Acts 2:1.

The growth of the Church: "The Lord added to the Church daily such as should be saved." Acts 2:47.

"Lord, lay not this sin to their charge." Acts 7:60.

. . . .

Explain the following terms: *Apostle, Pentecost, martyr, deacon, alms, believe, intent,* and *church.*

Identify Ananias, Sapphira, Saul, Barnabas, Gamaliel, and Matthias.

Lesson XIX

The Early Church (A.D. 37-40) (continued)

II. The Church Extended (Read Acts 8:1 to 12:25.)

    A. Persecution.

        1. What was the effect of Saul's persecution of the Church? Acts 8:3, 4.

        2. How did this persecution help to carry out the Great Commission? Matthew 28:18-20.

        3. Why did Philip, the deacon, leave Jerusalem? Acts 8:4, 5.

        4. Tell of Philip's work in Samaria and of the convert, Simon the sorcerer. Acts 8:5-25.

        5. How did the Ethiopian eunuch become a member of the Church? Acts 8:26-29.

        6. Read of Paul's conversion (A. D. 37). Acts 9:1-19. (Note how Paul's persecution of the Church was instrumental in bringing about his own conversion.)

        7. Why were the Jews so determined to kill Paul after he was converted? Acts 9:22-24, 29.

        8. Why did Paul go to Tarsus? Acts 9:29, 30; Acts 22:18, 21.

    B. The Gospel Given to the Gentiles.

        1. Trace the activities for Peter from Lydda to Joppa. Acts 9:32-43.

        2. What agencies were used in the conversion of Cornelius, the devout man? Acts 10.

        3. How did Peter explain to the Jews in the Church in Jerusalem his preaching of the Gospel to the Gentiles? Acts 11:1-18.

C. The Church Spread Beyond Palestine.
1. What regions beyond Palestine had now received the Gospel? Acts 11:19-21.
2. Were Jews and Gentiles alike receiving the Gospel in these places? Acts 11:19, 20.
3. Why did the Church in Jerusalem send Barnabas to Antioch of Syria? Acts 11:20-24.
4. Where have we previously met Barnabas? Acts 4:36, 37; 9:27; 12:1-19.
5. What follow-disciple helped Barnabas for a year in Antioch? Acts 11:25, 26.
6. Where were the disciples of Christ first called Christians? Acts 11:26.
7. Why did the Church of Antioch send Paul and Barnabas to Jerusalem at this time? Acts 11:27-30.
8. Tell of the renewed persecution in Jerusalem at this time. Acts 12:1-19.
9. What incident checked this persecution? Acts 12:20-23.
10. Did this persecution stop the growth of the Church? Acts 12:24-25.

Memorize:

The beginning words of the first sermon to the Gentiles:

"Of a truth I perceive that God is no respecter of persons: But in every nation he that feareth him, and worketh righteousness, is accepted with him." Acts 10:34-35.

Quotations for careful study:

New name for the disciples: "And the disciples were called Christians first at Antioch." Acts 11:26.

. . . .

Locate Antioch, Tarsus, Lydda, Joppa, Damascus, Cyprus.

Explain the following terms: *Christian, dispersion, exorcist, Grecian.*

Identify Philip, Ananias, John Mark, Cornelius, James.

Lesson XX

The Mission to the Gentiles

III. The Church Abroad

    A. First Missionary Journey of Paul (A.D. 48-50) (Acts 13, 14)

        1. Paul and Barnabas set apart by the Church in Antioch of Syria. Acts 13:1-4.
        Why did they go on this journey?

        2. Stop at Paphos after crossing through Cyprus. Acts 13:6-12.
            a. Who was converted here? Acts 13:6, 7.
            b. Why was Elimas struck blind? Acts 13:8-12.
            c. Saul is called Paul for the first time. Acts 13:9.

        3. Sail to Perga. Acts 13:13.
        Who, of their company, returned to Jerusalem?

        4. Go to Antioch of Pisidia. Acts 13:14-52.
            a. Paul's first recorded sermon.
                (1) Why was Paul ready to speak? Acts 13:16.
                (2) Why did he rehearse Jewish history? Acts 13:17-23.
                (3) What was the attitude of the Gentiles toward Paul's preaching? Acts 13:42
                (4) Note the change in attitude of the Jews. Acts 13:43-45.
                (5) Note the boldness of Paul and Barnabas. Acts 13:46.
            b. Why did Paul and Barnabas shake off the dust of their feet? Acts 13:51; Matthew 10:14.

        5. Go to Iconium. Acts 14:1-6.
        What trouble did the unbelieving Jews cause?

        6. Flee to Lystra. Acts 14:8-20.
            a. Why did the people think Paul and Barnabas were gods? Acts 14:7-12.
            b. Why were the missionaries so opposed to having sacrifices offered to them? Acts 14:12-17.
            c. Why was Paul stoned? Acts 14:18, 19.

7. Go to Derbe. Acts 14:20, 21.
   What did Paul and Barnabas do at Derbe?

8. Return by way of Lystra, Iconium, Antioch, Perga. Went to Attalia and sailed back to Antioch of Syria. Acts 14:21-26.
   What was the purpose of returning through these places? Acts 14:22, 23.

9. Report to the Church at Antioch. Acts 14:27, 28.
   What did they report?

10. Attend the Council in Jerusalem (A.D. 50). Read Acts 15:1-31.

   a. Who caused a dispute in the Church at Antioch? Acts 15:1a.

   b. What was the controversy about? Acts 15:1.

   c. Why were Paul and Barnabas sent to the Church at Jerusalem? Acts 15:2-4. (Titus went also. Galatians 2:1)

   d. Who contended for circumcision? Acts 15:5.

   e. What was Peter's statement concerning the matter? Acts 15:6-11.

   f. Who was James and what was his decision? Acts 15:13-21; Galatians 2:9.

   g. Was their decision the decision of the Lord? Acts 15:28; John 16:13.

   h. What was the effect of this letter and exhortation on the Church? Acts 15:30-34.

   i. Did this end the controversy over circumcision? Acts 15:31; Galatians 5:6; Galatians 6:16; Colossians 3:11.

Quotations for careful study:

"God made choice among us, that the Gentiles by my mouth should hear the word of the gospel and believe." Acts 15:17.

. . . .

Locate Antioch and Lystra.

Explain *ordain* and *confirm*.

Identify Timothy, James, Titus, and Cephas.

Lesson XXI

The Mission to the Gentiles (continued)

B. Second Missionary Journey of Paul (A.D. 51-54). Read Acts 15:36 to 18:23.

1. Antioch.
   a. Why did Paul go on this journey? Acts 15:36.
   b. Whom did Paul choose to accompany him? Acts 15:40.

2. Syria and Cilicia.
   What type of work did they do in these regions? Acts 15:41.

3. Lystra.
   a. Who joined Paul and Silas in Lystra? Acts 16:1.
   b. What do we know of this young man? Acts 16:1-3. II Timothy 1:5, 3:15; I Timothy 1:3.
   c. What were "the decrees" delivered to the Churches? Acts 16:4.

4. Phygia and Galatia.
   They went throughout these regions; desired to go west into Asia; were forbidden by the Holy Ghost. Acts 16:6.

5. Mysia.
   The desired to go north into Bithynia, but were forbidden by the Holy Ghost. Acts 16:7.

6. Troas.
   a. What was the "Macedonian Call"? Acts 16:9.
   b. What was the result of this vision? Acts 16:10.

7. Philippi (chief city of that part of Macedonia)
   a. Conversion of Lydia (first European convert) Who was Lydia? Acts 16:13-15.
   b. Conversion of the jailer.
      (1) Why were Paul and Silas cast into prison? Acts 16:16-22.
      (2) What happened while they were in prison? Acts 16:25-31.

(3) Why do you think the jailer asked Paul and Silas what to do to be saved?

(4) What was Paul's answer? Acts 16:31.

(5) What did Paul and Silas do that they might believe? Acts 16:32.

(6) What climaxed this? Acts 16:33.

8. Thessalonica.

What was the result of Paul's preaching here? Acts. 17:4-10.

9. Berea, Acts 17:10-15.

a. Why was Paul sent away? Acts 17:13, 14.

b. Who were left in Berea? Acts 17:14.

10. Athens.

Paul's sermon on Mars Hill.

(1) What suggested the subject for the sermon? Acts 17:16.

(2) Who invited Paul to preach? Acts 17:18.

(3) Give the substance of the sermon. Acts 17:22-31.

(4) How was his sermon received? Acts 17:32-34.

11. Corinth

a. Name some of Paul's associates here. Acts 18:2, 3, 5.

b. What letters did Paul write as a result of Timothy's report ? I Thessalonians 3:2; 5-10; II Thessalonians 1:1; II Thessalonians 2:2.

c. How was Paul encouraged to continue his work here? Acts 18:9, 10.

d. How long did he stay in Corinth? Acts 18:11, 18.

e. Tell of Paul's being taken before Gallio. Acts 18:12-16.

12. Ephesus.

Why did Paul not stay longer in Ephesus? Acts 18:19-21.

13. Caesarea.

Paul apparently goes from Caesarea to Jerusalem for the feast, as he had planned. Acts 18:21.

14. Antioch of Syria.
   No doubt Paul made a report of his work to the Church in Antioch as he did on his return from his first missionary tour—"he spent some time there." Acts 18:23.

Memorize:

For what were the people of Berea commended?

"These were more noble than those in Thessalonica, in that they received the word with all readiness of mind, and searched the scriptures daily, whether those things were so." Acts 17:11.
. . . .

Locate Troas, Philippi, Berea, Thessalonica, Athens, Corinth, and Ephesus.

Explain the following terms: *epistle, Areopagus, idol, idolatry, devout, "decrees", "Macedonian Call."*

Identify Silas, Lydia, Priscilla, and Aquilla.

Lesson XXII

The Mission to the Gentiles (continued)

C. Third Missionary Journey of Paul (A.D. 54-58).
   Read Acts 18:23 to 21:15.

   1. Antioch of Syria.
      Paul leaves Antioch for the third time on a missionary tour. Acts 18:23a.

   2. Galatia and Phrygia.
      Why did Paul go through these regions again? Acts 18:23b.

   3. Ephesus.
      a. What teacher preceded Paul in Ephesus? Acts 18:24.
      b. What was wrong with his teaching? Acts 18:25.
      c. Who "expounded unto him the way of God more perfectly"? Acts 18:26.
      d. Why was the baptism of John not valid in Paul's time? Acts 19:3-5.
      e. Did the gift of the Holy Spirit precede or follow baptism? Acts 19:5-6.

    f. Why did Paul separate himself and disciples, after three months, from the Jews? Acts 19.

    g. Where did Paul then teach? Acts 19:9, 10.

    h. What led to the confession of the exorcists and to the burning of their books? Acts 19:13-19:8, 9.

    i. What was the cause of Demetrius's complaint? Acts 19:23-27.

    j. Show the tact and good judgment that the town clerk exercised in dispersing the mob. Acts 19:35-41.

    k. What letter did Paul write during his stay in Ephesus? II Corinthians 7:8-12.

4. Macedonia.

    a. From II Corinthians 2:13 we learn that Paul left Ephesus and came to Troas hoping to meet Titus to get a report on the response of his first epistle to the Church at Corinth. Disappointed in not finding him there, he went on to Macedonia and there met Titus and learned for the first time that his epistle had been well received. II Corinthians 7:6-8.

    b. Paul writes his second letter to the Church at Corinth, defending his apostleship to pave the way for his next visit to them. II Corinthians.

5. Greece.

    a. How long does Paul stay this time in Corinth? Acts 20:3.

    b. What letter did he write while here? Romans.

6. Macedonia.

Paul goes back through Macedonia; leaves Philippi after the days of unleavened bread. Acts 20:3-6.

7. Troas.

    a. What was the primary object of the disciples' coming together, when Paul preached to them? Acts 20:7.

    b. What happened to Eutychus here? Acts 20:7, 8.

8. Journey to Miletus.
   a. This part of the journey was made partly on foot, and partly by ship off the west coast of Asia Minor. Acts 20:13-15.
   b. What was Paul's message to the elders from Ephesus? Acts 20:17-35.
   c. Why did he dare go to Jerusalem, after being warned? Acts 20:22, 24.
   d. Why such sorrow at parting? Acts 20:37, 38.
9. Journey from Miletus to Jerusalem.
   a. What was the general course of the journey? Acts 21: 2, 3, 8-15.
   b. What was the warning of Agabus to Paul? Acts 21:10, 11.

Memorize:

What does Acts 17:26 teach concerning the brotherhood of man?

"And hath made of one blood all nations of men for to dwell on all the face of the earth, and hath determined the times before appointed, and the bounds of their habitation."

Quotation for careful study:

"It is more blessed to give than to receive." Acts 20:35.

. . . .

Locate Galatia and Phrygia.
Explain *divination*.
Identify Diana, Apollos, Luke, Eutychus, and Demetrius.

Lesson XXIII

Paul from Jerusalem to Rome

D. Events Leading up to Paul's Fourth Journey (Read Acts 21:15 to 28:32.)
   1. At Jerusalem (A.D. 58)
      a. How was Paul received by the brethren? Acts 21:17-20.
      b. How was Paul received by the Jews? Acts 21:27-31.
      c. By whom was Paul rescued? Acts 21:31-34.
      d. Read Paul's speech to the mob. Acts 22:1-21.

    e. According to Paul, when did he receive his commission to the Gentiles? Acts 22:17-21.

    f. Read of Paul's trial before Ananias. Acts 22:30..

    g. Why was it necessary to remove Paul from Jerusalem to Caesarea? Acts 23:11-23.

2. At Caesarea.

    a. By whom was Paul first accused? Acts 24:27.

    b. How did Paul's defense affect Felix? Acts 24:22-27.

    c. How long did Paul remain in Caesarea? Acts 24:27.

    d. Who replaced Felix? Acts 24:27.

    e. Tell of Festus's treatment of Paul. Acts 24:1-12.

    f. What effect did Paul's defense have on Agrippa? Acts 26:1-29.

3. The purpose of the Journey.

    a. When Paul was in Corinth he wrote what promise to the Romans? Romans 15:24, 25, 28.

    b. When and where did Paul receive God's will concerning his trip to Rome? Acts 23:10, 11.

    c. What appeal did Paul make which determined how he should go to Rome? Acts 25:11, 12.

E. The Fourth Journey (A.D. 61)

1. Who accompanied Paul on this Journey? Acts 27:1, 2.

2. At Sidon, how was Paul treated? Acts 27:3.

3. What advice did Paul give at Fair Havens? Acts 27:9, 10.

4. What happened as the result of the disregard of Paul's advice by Julius? Acts 27:9-44.

5. How did Paul help the people of the island of Melita? Acts 28:1-11.

6. Where did the journey end? Acts 28:13.

F. Paul in Rome (A.D. 62-63)

1. How was Paul received? Acts 28:14, 15.

2. Where did he stay in Rome? How long? Acts 28:30.

3. How did Paul occupy himself as a prisoner? Acts 28:17-29. (Paul probably wrote four epistles while in prison at this time, namely: Ephesians, Philippians, Colossians, and Philemon.)

4. What more do we know of Paul?
   a. While in prison, received help from the Church in Philippi. Philippians 1:5; 4:22.
   b. Visits the Church in Crete. Titus 1:5.
   c. Returns to Ephesus for the third time. I Timothy 1:3.
   d. His confidence in Mark restored. Acts 15:36-41; II Timothy 4:11.
   e. Desires Timothy to bring him his cloak, books and parchments. II Timothy 4:13.
   f. Finished his course. Acts 20:24; II Timothy 4:6-8.

Memorize:

Why did Paul expect a crown of righteousness?

"I have fought a good fight, I have finished my course, I have kept the faith: Henceforth there is laid up for me a crown of righteousness, which the Lord, the righteous judge, shall give me at that day: and not to me only, but unto all them also that love his appearing." II Timothy 4:7, 8.

Quotations for careful study:

"I would to God, that not only thou, but also all that hear me this day, were both almost, and altogether such as I am, except these bonds." Acts 26:29.

. . . .

Locate Melita and Rome.
Identify Felix, Festus, Agrippa, Bernice, and Caesar.

PART THREE
LETTERS AND REVELATION

INTRODUCTION

The Epistles were written to missionary congregations of Christian converts or to individuals, upon different occasions. There is throughout them an entire agreement both as to facts and doctrines. They constitute, when taken together, an invaluable commentary on the practical and doctrinal meaning of the life and teachings of Christ.

I and II Thessalonians were probably written during the second missionary journey; I and II Corinthians, Romans, and possibly Galatians were written during the third journey; Philippians, Colossians, Ephesians, Philemon, from Rome during the two years in Paul's own house; I Timothy and Titus from Corinth after the trial in Rome and acquittal; II Timothy in Rome during the second imprisonment and just before the martyrdom.

The Letters are taken up in this division in what is thought to be the most commonly accepted chronological order. It should be stated, however, that there is no general agreement as to the exact dates at which many of the letters were written. Teachers who prefer the King James arrangement may have their pupils follow this order in their study of Part Three.

The outlines, notes, and questions on the different letters should be regarded as purely tentative and suggestive. Teachers will, of course, use and supplement these outlines as they deem proper. In the study of each letter pupils should be required to learn the author, to whom written, and the purpose or general theme. For review, it will be well to group letters by authors and types.

Lesson XXIV

I Thessalonians

I Thessalonians was written by Paul at Corinth about A.D. 50, a short time after the church was established at Thessalonica. His main object is to answer the questions he had received from them by Timothy, mainly on the second coming of the Lord. They seem to have had the mistaken idea that the Lord would return very soon and to fear that those who had died might not have a part in His coming. He also gives various exhortations to remain true to his teachings in spite of persecutions and false teachings.

I. Salutation. (1:1)

II. Thanksgiving. (1:2 to 3:10)
1. How did the people at Thessalonica receive the gospel? (1:2-10)
2. What results did Paul have in his teachings? (2:1-10)
3. How did Paul communicate with them? (2:7 to 3:10)

III. Prayer. (3:11-13)

IV. Body of the Letter.
1. What does Paul teach concerning brotherly love? (4:9-12)
2. Where shall all the dead and the living meet the Lord when He comes? (4:13-18) (I Cor. 15:50-52)
3. When shall we expect His coming? (5:1-3)
4. Various exhortations.
   a. From what are we to abstain? (5:21)
   b. To what shall we hold fast? (5:22)

V. Benediction. (5:23-24)

Memorize:

Good and evil: "Prove all things; hold fast that which is good. Abstain from all appearance of evil." I Thessalonians 5:21, 22.

. . . .

Explain the term, *exhort.*

Lesson XXV

II Thessalonians

II Thessalonians was written only a short time after I Thessalonians, A.D. 50, and probably from Corinth also. In this epistle Paul corrects some of the misunderstandings caused by his first letter concerning the return of the Lord, or by a forged letter, "as from us" (2:2), saying "that the day of Christ is at hand."

I. Salutation. (1:1-2)

II. Thanksgiving. (1:3-12)
(For faith, love and patience)

III. The Body of the Letter.

1. Upon whom will the Lord send his vengeance? (1:7-8)

2. What will precede the second coming of the Lord? (2:1-3)

3. What description is given of the man of sin? (2:4-11)

4. Exhortations. (3:6-15) How did Paul admonish the idle?

IV. Benediction and Salutation. (3:16-19)

Lesson XXVI

Galatians

Galatians was written by Paul to the churches in Galatia, a district of the Roman Empire. From all indications, it was written about A.D. 52 from either Ephesus, Macedonia, or Corinth while he was on the third missionary journey. The first portion is spent in defending his right to preach the gospel. In chapters 3 and 4 he defends the gospel against Judaizing teachers. The remainder of the letter is devoted mainly to practical duties which grow out of the gospel.

I. Salutation. (1:1-5)

II. The theme of the Gospel. (1:1-10)

III. The body of the letter.

1. Paul's defense.

a. From what source did Paul's authority come? (1:11-12)

b. Study Paul's autobiography. (1:13-24)

c. What was the decision of the Jerusalem council? (2:7-10)

d. Why did Paul rebuke Peter? (2:12-20)

2. Doctrinal Instructions. Chapters 2, 3, 4) (Paul defends the Gospel.)

a. How is justification obtained? (3:24)

b. How do the Gentiles become heirs of the promise of Abraham? (3:23-29)

      c. What allegory was used to show the relation of the law to faith? (4:21-31)

  3. Exhortations and practical applications.

      a. Why do we seek justification by faith rather than by the law? (5:1-4)

      b. What are the works of the flesh; and what is the fruit of the Spirit? (5:16-26)

      c. What is our two-fold responsibility? (6:2-5)

  4. How did Paul suffer for Jesus Christ? (6:17)

IV. Benediction. (6:18)

Memorize:

The fruit of the Spirit: "But the fruit of the Spirit is love, joy, peace, longsuffering, gentleness, goodness, faith, meekness, temperance: against such there is no law." Galatians 5:22, 23.

What may we expect to harvest? "Be not deceived; God is not mocked: for whatsoever a man soweth, that shall he also reap." Galatians 6:7.

. . . .

Explain the term, *justify.*

Lesson XXVII

I Corinthians

The church was established at Corinth by Paul about A.D. 55. Corinth was a commercial center whose inhabitants comprised almost all nationalities. They were schooled in Greek philosophy and lived a very impure life. After Paul left Corinth, the church became divided over leaders and some other matters. Paul, while in Ephesus, received reports concerning these difficulties and wrote I Corinthians to correct their errors. The first four chapters are devoted to the correction of the dissensions. The remainder of the book gives a discussion on marriage, the Lord's Supper, worship and assembly, and the resurrection.

  I. Greeting. (1:1-3)

  II. Thanksgiving. (1:4-9)

  III. Body of the Letter.

1. What division did Paul find in the Corinthian Church? (1:10-13)
2. How did Paul condemn such division? (1:13-17)
3. What two sins were condemned in the Corinthian Church? (Chapters 5-6)
4. How did Paul reaffirm Christ's teaching on divorce? (7:10-11) (Matthew 19:9)
5. What does Paul teach in regard to offending another? (8:13)
6. What use does Paul make for the old testament scriptures? (10:11)
7. In what manner and for what purpose do we keep the Lord's Supper? (11:23-29)
8. What is Paul's teaching on the relationship of individuals to the church? (12:12-27)
9. What is man's greatest virtue? (13)
10. Unto what end should each act of worship lead? (14:12-17)
11. How does Paul prove a resurrection of the Christian's body? (15:20-23)
12. How are the dead raised up and with what body do they come? (15:35-58)
13. What is the basis of Christian giving? (16:1-9)

IV. Benediction. (16:19-23)

Memorize:

"Though I speak with the tongues of men and of angels, and have not charity, I am become as sounding brass, or a tinkling cymbal.

"And though I have the gift of prophecy, and understand all mysteries, and all knowledge; and though I have all faith, so that I could remove mountains, and have not charity, I am nothing.

"And though I bestow all my goods to feed the poor, and though I give my body to be burned, and have not charity, it profiteth me nothing.

"Charity suffereth long, and is kind; charity envieth not; charity vaunteth not itself, is not puffed up.

"Doth not behave itself unseemly, seeketh not her own, is not easily provoked, thinketh no evil;

"Rejoiceth not in inquity, but rejoiceth in the truth;

"Beareth all things, believeth all things, hopeth all things, endureth all things.

"Charity never faileth; but whether there be prophecies, they shall fail; whether there be tongues, they shall cease; whether there be knowledge, it shall vanish away.

"For we know in part, and we prophesy in part.

"But when that which is perfect is come, then that which is in part shall be done away.

"When I was a child, I spake as a child, I understood as a child, I thought as a child: but when I became a man, I put away childish things.

"For now we see through a glass darkly; but then face to face: now I know in part; but then I shall know even as also I am known.

"And now abideth faith, hope, charity, these three; but the greatest of these is charity." I Corinthians 13.

Quotations for careful study:

"Eye hath not seen, nor ear heard, neither have entered into the heart of man, the things which God hath prepared for them that love Him." I Corinthians 2:9.

"But take heed lest by any means this liberty of yours become a stumbling block to them that are weak." I Corinthians 8:9.

. . . .

Explain the following terms: *subvert, reprobate, prophesy, immortal.*

Lesson XXVIII

II Corinthians

II Corinthians was written by Paul a short time after I Corinthians, about the year A.D. 57 from Macedonia. This letter was written mainly to express his joys over the better state of things in the church as a result of the first letter, and to defend his apostleship. He also uses this opportunity to convey further counsels.

I. Greetings. (1:1-11)

II. Maintenance of Paul's apostleship.
   1. Paul's defense against the church of being unreliable. How would Paul's discipline have brought sorrow to the Corinthians, if he had done there as he promised? (1:23-2:2)
   2. Paul's apostolic office.
      a. What apostle commended Paul as an apostle of Christ? (Acts 9:27; II Corinthians 1:1)
      b. What ministry was committed to the Apostle Paul? (5:18-21)
   3. Collection for the Jerusalem Church.
      a. How does the Lord repay us for our generosity? (9:6-10)
      b. For whom did Paul ask this bounty? (9:12-13)
   4. A measure of true service.
      a. Against what things did Paul make war? (10:3-6)
      b. What signs proved Paul's sincerity? (11:22-28)
      c. What attitudes did Paul take toward his infirmaties? (12-10)
   5. Promise of third visit? (13:1-14)

III. Benediction (13:11-14)

Quotations for careful study:

The basis of Christian giving: "Upon the first day of the week let every one of you lay by him in store, as God hath prospered him." I Corinthians 16:2.

The basis for Christian reward: "He which soweth sparingly shall reap also sparingly; and he which soweth bountifully shall reap also bountifully." II Corinthians 9:6.

Lesson XXIX

Romans

Romans was written by Paul in A.D. 57 from Corinth. The purpose of this letter was to set forth the great doctrines of Christianity, for there had been no apostle in Rome to preach the Gospel. This letter would also prepare the way for

Paul, who had a desire to go to Rome. The power of the Gospel is set forth in the first eleven chapters. Chapters 12 to 16 explain the principles of Christian life.

I. Salutation. (1:1-7)

II. Thanksgiving. (1:8-15)

III. Body of the Letter.

    1. Doctrinal.

        a. What is God's plan for man's salvation (1:16-17)

        b. What is the ground for God's judgment of all men? (2:12-13)

        c. How does Paul prove the guilt of all divisions of the human race? (1:18-3:20)

        d. What provisions has God made to save all? (3:21-25)

        e. What benefits accrue to the saved? (5:1-11)

        f. What obedience had freed the Romans from sin? (6:17, 3-5)

        g. What illustration did Paul use to show that the law of Christ supersedes the law of Moses? (7:2-6)

        h. Who are the sons of God and how are they made so? (8:14-17)

    2. Explanatory.

        a. Why did the Gentiles attain to righteousness? Why did Israel fail? (9:30-31)

        b. How is faith obtained? (10-17)

        c. How are both Jews and Gentiles to stand or fall? (11:19-23)

    3. Exhortations and practical advice.

        a. What is to be the Christian's attitude toward governments? (13:1-7)

        b. All are to live and die "unto" whom? Why? (14:8-9)

        c. What are the responsibilities of those who are strong in Christ? (15:1-3)

IV. Benediction. (16:1-27)

Memorize:

The penalty for sin and the gift of God contrasted: "For the wages of sin is death; but the gift of God is eternal life through Jesus Christ our Lord." Romans 6:23.

Reasonable service: "I beseech you therefore, brethren, by the mercies of God, that ye present your bodies a living sacrifice, holy, acceptable unto God, which is your reasonable service. And be not conformed to this world: but be ye transformed by the renewing of your mind, that ye may prove what is that good, and acceptable, and perfect, will of God." Romans 12:1-2.

Quotations for careful study:

"For I am not ashamed of the gospel of Christ; for it is the power of God unto salvation to every one that believeth; to the Jew first, and also to the Greek." Romans 1:16.

"The powers that be are ordained of God." Romans 13:1.

What fulfills the law? "Owe no man anything, but love one another." Romans 13:8.

. . . .

Explain the terms: *chaste* and *amen.*

Lesson XXX

Colossians

Colossians was written by Paul from Rome about A.D. 62 while he was in prison. He meets the errors of Judaizing teachers by taking his stand upon the doctrine of the person of Christ. He shows how Christ is the one mediator between God and man, thus excluding angel worship and ceremonies. Likeness to Him is the one great source of sanctification.

I. Greetings. (1:2)

II. Thanksgiving. (1:3-12)

III. The body of the letter—doctrinal

    1. How did Paul set forth the preeminence of Christ? (1:13-20)

    2. In whom were they circumcised? How was it done? (2:11-13)

3. What was accomplished in the death of Christ? (2:14-15)

4. What was to be put to death and what was to be put on? (3:5-14)

5. How was the word to dwell in them? How manifested? (3:16-17)

6. What was to be the relationship of wives to husbands; husbands to wives; parents to children; servants to masters; masters to servants? (3:18-25, 4:1)

IV. Benediction. (4:7-18)

Quotations for careful study:
Where should Christians center their affections? "Set your affections on things above, not on things on the earth." Colossians 3:2.

. . . .

Explain the terms, *preeminence* and *barbarians.*

Lesson XXXI

Philemon

The epistle to Philemon was written by Paul about the year A.D. 62. It is one of the four personal letters written by Paul. Its purpose is to create a better relation between a runaway slave and his master. It illustrates Christian love and sympathy in action in the ordinary affairs of life.

I. Greetings. (1-3)

II. Thanksgiving and Prayer. (4-7)

III. Body of the Letter.

   1. Plea for Onesimus.

     a. What change had Onesimus experienced since running away from his master? (8-10)

     b. Who sent him back to his master? (12-14)

     c. What is the new relation to exist between Onesimus and Philemon? (15-18)

     d. What sacrifice was Paul willing to make for Onesimus? (18-19)

IV. Greetings to Persons. (23-24)

V. Benediction. (25)

Lesson XXXII

Philippians

The church at Philippi was established by Paul about A.D. 50 or 51. It is interesting to note the fact that this was the first congregation of Christians that ever existed on the soil of Europe. The letter to the Philippians was written by Paul about A.D. 63 and carried to them by Epaphroditus. It is an outpouring of the love and affectionate tenderness of Paul to the Philippians.

I. Greetings (1:1-2)

II. Thanksgivings (1:3-8) and Prayer. (1:9-11)

III. The Body of the Letter.

    1. Living a holy life.

        a. What relation does Christ sustain to the life of Paul? (1:20-26)

        b. How does Paul teach unity? (2:1-5)

        c. How does Paul illustrate the lowly mind? (2:6-11)

    2. The resurrection.

        a. What does Paul consider his aim or prize? (3:11)

        b. Where does Paul look for his prize? (3:13-14)

        c. What change shall be made in our bodies at the resurrection? (3:21)

    3. Exhortations for Christian life.
        a. What does Paul teach on anxiety? (4:6)
        b. How does God keep our hearts and minds? (4:7-9)

IV. Parting salutation. (4:21-23)

Memorize:

Upon what should Christians meditate? "Finally, brethren, whatsoever things are true, whatsoever things are honest, whatsoever things are just, whatsoever things are pure, whatsoever things are lovely, whatsoever things are of good report; if there be any virtue, and if there be any praise, think on these things." Philippians 4:8.

Lesson XXXIII

Ephesians

The Book of Ephesians was written by Paul about the year A.D. 62 while he was in prison at Rome. Paul established the Church at Ephesus while on the second missionary journey, and spent about three years there while on the third journey. It is possible that this letter was written to meet certain difficulties that arose in the church.

I. Salutation. (1:1-2)

II. Thanksgiving and Prayer. (1:16:23)

    1. What was the specific work of God in Salvation? (1:3-14)

    2. What actions did God bring about by the power which was wrought in Christ? (1:19-23)

    3. For whom does Paul pray? (3:14-21)

III. Body of the Letter.

    1. Jews and Gentiles *one* in Christ.

        a. What was our spiritual condition before Christ came? (2:1-3)

        b. What is the gift of God by which we are saved? (2:8-9)

        c. What is the Holy Temple composed of? (2:19-22)

    2. Unity of the Church.

        a. What are the seven bonds of unity? (4:3-6)

        b. In what ways were the Gentiles called from their former life to a new life? (4:22-32)

    3. Sundry duties and exhortations.

        a. In what shall the fruit of the Spirit be found? (5:9-10)

        b. What is the similarity of relationship between the husband and the wife and Christ and the Church? (5:33)

        c. What are the mutual duties of parents and children? (6:1-4)

        d. What is the whole armor of God? (6:10-23)

IV. Benediction. (6:24)

Quotations for careful study:

How may one resist temptation? "Put on the whole armor of God that ye may be able to stand against the wiles of the devil." Ephesians 6:11.

"Children, obey your parents in the Lord: for this is right. Honor thy father and thy mother; which is the first command with promise." Ephesians 6:1, 2.

Lesson XXXIV

Hebrews

It is generally considered that the Book of Hebrews was written from Italy by the Apostle Paul between the years 63 and 65 A.D. However, there is some difference of opinion as to the authorship of Hebrews, since there is no inscription or salutation found in the letter. The people to whom it was sent were the Jewish Christians of Judea who were facing a state of apostasy because of persecution and imminent danger of the destruction of Jerusalem. It is a summary of the Gospel and the completion of the law. The author, by many illustrations and examples from the old law, demonstrates the superiority of the new covenant to the Law of Moses.

It was difficult for the Jew to realize that the Law of Moses was fulfilled by Christ and taken out of the way. There was a tendency among them to try to hold to the Law while professing to follow Christ.

I. The Proposition: The Majesty and Pre-eminence of Christ. (1-3)

   1. Through whom does God reveal his word to men in this day (age)? (1-2)

   2. In what way is Christ superior to angels? (1-4 and 5)

   3. How did God confirm Christ's word which is superior to that of the angels? (1:4-5)

   4. What nature did Christ assume and why? (2:16-18)

II. Arguments: The Law of Christ Superior to That of Moses. (3-13)

   1. How were Moses and Christ contrasted in regard to God's house? (3:5-6)

   2. What is the fullness of the power of God's word? (4:12-13)

3. What were the duties of the high priest and how could Christ serve this capacity better than the Mosaic high priests? (5:1-2) (4:15)

4. How may we be guilty of the crucifixion of our Lord? (6:4-6)

5. Christ is the fulfillment of what immutable promise? (6:13:20)

6. What is the similarity of the priesthood of Christ and Melchisedec? (7:1-8)

7. Why was the law disannulled and the priesthood changed? (7:11-12; 18-19)

8. With the change of priesthood, what change was made in the law? (Chapter 8)

9. When and by what was the New Testament made effective? (9:16-17)

10. Why was there a change of will, and upon what was the second established? (10:7-10)

11. How are we to draw near unto God? (10:22-25)

12. Compare the punishment of disobedience under the old law and the new covenant? (10:26-30)

13. Give your favorite example of faith as listed in the eleventh chapter.

14. What should be our reaction to these examples? (12:1-2)

III. Sundry Exhortations. (Chapter 13)

Memorize:

Faith defined: "Now faith is the substance of things hoped for, the evidence of things not seen." Hebrews 11:1.

. . . .

Explain the terms, *covenant, anchor,* and *Antichrist.*

Lesson XXXV

I Peter

I Peter is one of the most beautiful of the New Testament writings. It is not philosophical nor profound, but it is full of the spirit of Christian devotion. The letter is addressed "to the elect sojourners of the Dispersion, in Pontus, Galatia,

Cappadocia, Asia, and Bithynia" (1:1). These regions are in the northern part of Asia Minor and border on the Black Sea. This letter is usually attributed to Peter and is supposed to have been written about 64 A.D. There are, however, several references in the epistle to persecutions suffered by the Christians which may have occurred during the reign of Domitian between 81 and 96 A.D. Hence modern authorities place the date of the letter as late as 90 to 95 A.D. and ascribe its authorship to some one other than the Apostle Peter.

I. Greetings (1:1-2)

II. Thanksgiving for the privileges which Christians enjoy, even in the midst of tribulation (1:3-12)

III. Jesus as the supreme example (1:13-25)

IV. The Christian as God's spiritual temple (2:1-10)

V. Detailed directions as to conduct, enforced by the example of Christ

1. Introductory summary (2:11-12)

2. Obedience to earthly authority (2:13-17)

3. Faithfulness of slaves; Christ their example (2:18-25)

4. Conduct of wives and husbands (3:1-7)

5. Brotherhood among the believers (3:8-12)

6. Christ's example, an inspiration to pure living (3:13-4:11)

VI. Further detailed directions

1. Suffering for Christ a privilege (4:12-19)

2. Urging pastors to live exemplary lives (5:1-4)

3. Exhorting young men to humility and faith (5:5-6)

4. Resisting the Tempter by alertness (5:7-11)

VII. Salutation. (5:12-14)

Questions—Lesson XXXV.

1. On what is hope of immortality based? (1:3; 18-23)

2. To what end is our faith tested? (1:7-9)

3. What are Christians exhorted to do? (1:13-16, 22)

4. How enduring is the Word of the Lord? (1:25)

5. Are Christians to obey civil law? (2:13-17)
6. What is said about those who "love life?" (3:10-12)
7. What is said about those who suffer for Christ? (3:17; 4:16)
8. What is the test of stewardship? (4:10)

. . . .

Explain the term, *emulation.*

Lesson XXXVI

James

This Epistle opens with the words, "James, a servant of God and of the Lord Jesus Christ, to the twelve tribes who are of the Dispersion, greeting." This is the only place where the writer makes any reference to himself, but the epistle has long been ascribed to James, the brother of Jesus, who became a leader in the Church at Jerusalem. There is no definite indication of its time of writing. The usually accepted date is A.D. 40 to 50, but more recent authorities think that the probable date is between A.D. 70 to 100. "To the twelve tribes of the Dispersion" cannot, in a literal sense, be taken to indicate the destination of the epistle since the twelve tribes had long ago disappeared. This is the author's way of saying that this letter is to be read to all the churches.

   I. Salutation (1:1)

  II. Testing of faith and character (1:2-19)

 III. Faith accompanied by obedience (1:20-27)

  IV. Warning against subservience to the rich (2:1-13)

   V. Faith and works (2:14-16)

  VI. Need of self-control in speech (3:1-12)

 VII. Warning against strife; its origin in rivalry and love of pleasure (3:13-4:12)

VIII. The uncertainty of life (4:13-17)

  IX. Riches gained unjustly a curse (5:1-6)

   X. Exhortation to patience (5:7-11)

  XI. Miscellaneous exhortations (5:12-20)

Note: In reading this epistle note that it does not follow the usual form of a letter. Notice in particular the ending.

Questions—Lesson XXXVI.

1. What is the source of true wisdom? (1:5; 3:17)   Of good gifts? (1:17)
2. How is "pure religion" defined? (1:27)
3. What is said about faith without works? (2:14-18; 1:22)
4. How may we have a sense of God's presence? (4:7-8)
5. How does God regard our failure to do what we know to be right?   (4:17)
6. What promise is made about the prayer of a righteous person? (5:16) About one who is instrumental in converting a sinner from the error of his way?   (5:20)

Memorize:
What must we do besides hear? "But be ye doers of the word, and not hearers only, deceiving your own selves." James 1:22.

Quotations for careful study:
"Every good gift and every perfect gift is from above, and cometh down from the Father of lights." James 1:17.
"Resist the devil and he will flee from you."   James 4:7.

Lesson XXXVII

I Timothy

I Timothy was written by Paul to Timothy from Macedonia in A.D. 66 or 67, while Timothy was at Ephesus. Since this is a personal letter, it has a different atmosphere from those addressed to Churches. Paul left Timothy at Ephesus to have charge of the work there. Therefore, it is full of instructions applicable to preachers. The first chapter explains the assignment and the remaining chapters are filled with general instructions.

I. Greetings. (1:1-2)

II. Thanksgiving. (1:12-13)

III. Body of the Letter.
    1. Paul's assignment to Timothy.
       a. Why was Timothy left at Ephesus? (1:3-4)
       b. What is Paul's charge to Timothy? (1:18-19)

2. Paul's instructions to Timothy on
   a. Public worship.
      (1) For whom should prayer be offered? (2:1-8)
      (2) What instructions were given in regard to
           women's dress? (2:9) Teaching?
           (2:11-15)
   b. Bishops and deacons.
      (1) What instructions are given concerning
           qualities of elders? (3:1-7)
      (2) What instructions are given concerning
           qualification of deacons? (3:8-10)
      (3) Why did Paul give such instructions?
           (3:15-16)
   c. General conduct of the church.
      (1) What were the signs of apostasy as pro-
           phesied by Paul? (4:1-5)
      (2) Who are widows, and how should they be
           treated? (5:3-16)
      (3) With what earthly goods should we be con-
           tent? (6:6-8)
      (4) What instructions are given to the rich?
           (6:17-19)

IV. Salutation. (6:20-21)

Quotations for careful study:
"Let no man despise thy youth; but be thou an example
of the believers, in word, in conversation, in charity, in spirit,
in faith, in purity."   I Timothy 4:12.

Lesson XXXVIII

II Timothy

II Timothy was written by Paul while he was in prison at
Rome shortly before his death between A.D. 66 and 68. Since
this is the last message to Timothy Paul expected to write,
it is filled with solemn counsel, expectation, and final instructions to his son in the gospel.

I. Greetings. (1:1-2)

II. Thanksgiving. (1:3-5)

III. Body of the Letter.
Paul's directions to Timothy.
1. What should Timothy not be ashamed of? (1:8)
2. To what should Timothy hold fast? (1:13)
3. Why should Timothy study? (2:15-16)
4. What should Timothy follow? (2:22-23)
5. What are the conditions of which Paul spoke? (3:1-5)
6. For what purpose is all scripture given? (3:16-17)
7. What was Paul's last charge to Timothy? (4:1-5)
8. What is Paul's departing statement? (4:6-8)

IV. Parting salutations. (4:19-22)

Memorize:

The importance of study: "Study to show thyself approved unto God, a workman that needeth not to be ashamed, rightly dividing the word of truth." II Timothy 2:15.

. . . .

Explain the terms, *scripture* and *inspiration.*

Note: II Timothy 4:7, 8 was quoted for memory work in connection with the life of Paul in Lesson XXIII.

Lesson XXXIX

Titus

The epistle to Titus was written to him by Paul about A.D. 66 to 68, while Titus was in Crete. Paul left Titus in Crete for a purpose, and the letter gives instructions on carrying out his duties. Paul probably wrote this letter while in Macedonia at which time he expected to spend the winter in Nicopolis.

I. Opening Salutation. (1:1-4)

II. Body of the Letter.
1. Directions to Titus.
    a. Why did Paul leave Titus in Crete? (1:5)
    b. What are the qualities of an elder? (1:6-9)
    c. Whom did Paul rebuke? Why? (1:10-13)
    d. What practical duties was Titus to teach? (2:1-6)
    e. What message did Paul send to servants? (2:9-15)
2. Various exhortations and duties of Christians. (3:1-4)

III. Personal Directions. 3:12-14)

IV. Closing Salutation. (3:15)

Lesson XL

I John

As to form, I John can scarcely be regarded as an epistle, since it does not contain an address or salutation. The conditions which it seems to portray would indicate that it is written to the Christians of Asia Minor. The ideas expressed are very similar to those contained in the Gospel of John and it appears to have been written by the same author. The date of the Epistle is about A.D. 90. The purpose of the author is to bring reassurance to the people to whom he is writing. He does not claim to teach them anything new but reassures them of the things which they have already been taught (2:7; 2:20; 4:16; 5:13).

   I. Introduction—Eternal life manifested in Jesus (1:1-4)

  II. Some vivid contrasts (1:5-2:17)

 III. Warnings against false teachers (2:18-29)

 IV. God's children and their relationship to him (3:1-24)

  V. The duty of brotherly love (4:7-5:12)

 VI. Conclusion (5:13-21)

Questions—Lesson XL.

1. Give two terms which the writer used to describe or characterize God. (1:5; 4:7, 16)

2. What is the test of fellowship with God, or love for God? (1:6-7; 2:24; 3:24; 4:8; 20)

3. What evidence has the Christian of his acceptance with the Father? (3:14; 24; 5:10)

4. Cite quotations to show that love is the central theme of this epistle.

Quotations for careful study:

"We love Him because He first loved us." I John 4:19.

. . . .

Explain the term, *advocate.*

Lesson XLI

II John

The author of II John styles himself "The Elder." Tradition has called him John. Many of the early Church Fathers identified him as John the Presbyter in Ephesus. The letter is addressed to "The elect lady and her children," which is taken to mean that it was addressed to some church in Asia Minor. He is thinking of some church, for he warns the members of certain missionaries who plan to visit them teaching what he considers to be a false doctrine. It is an exhortation to love and perseverance.

I. Greeting (1:1-3)

II. Commendation and warning (1:4-7)

III. Simple fidelity to Christ (1:8-11)

IV. Conclusion (1:12-13)

Questions—Lesson XLI.

1. What, again, is the real test of love? (1:6)
2. To whom is the presence of the Father and the Son promised? (1:9)
3. Why did John not write a long letter? (1:12)

Lesson XLII

III John

This epistle is by the same author as the other two epistles bearing this name, but it is written to an individual—"My dear friend Gaius." The Elder commends Gaius for his work in caring for the traveling preachers and evangelists through the love gifts of the churches. The local leader in this church is the assuming Diotrephes. The date of the epistle is approximately A.D. 91.

I. Salutation and commendation of Gaius (1:1-4)

II. Praise of his piety and hospitality to the traveling ministers (1:5-8)

III. Denunciation of Diotrephes (1:9-11)

IV. Commendation of Demetrius (1:12)

V. Promise of a visit and greetings (1:13-14)

Questions—Lesson XLII.

1. Is this letter addressed to a church? (1:1)
2. What does the writer commend? (1:3-7)
3. What good wish is made for Gaius? (1:2)
4. Why, again, is the letter brief?

Lesson XLIII

Jude

The author of this epistle is Jude who designates himself "as a servant of Jesus Christ and the brother of James." Since Jude, or Judas, was a very common name among the Jews, it is difficult to identify the author. The time and the place of the writing are also uncertain. Some authorities place the date between 70 and 80 A.D.; others, as late as 125 A.D. The purpose of the letter is clearly stated in the third and fourth verses—a strong denunciation against the false teachings and gross immorality of certain church members who were slyly undermining the true teachings of Christianity. In this respect Jude bears a close resemblance to the second chapter of II Peter. The writer appears to be addressing his message not to any particular church or group but to Christians in general.

I. Salutation (1-2)

II. Purpose of letter (3-4)

III. Punishment of false teachers and evil doers (5-16)

IV. Exhortation to right faith and living (17-23)

V. Benediction (24-25)

Questions—Lesson XLIII.

1. Why was this epistle written? To whom?
2. Give some ancient examples of punishment for disobedience.
3. What exhortation is given to true Christians?

Quotations for careful study:
Benediction: "Now unto Him that is able to keep you from falling, and to present you faultless before the presence of His glory with exceeding joy,
"To the only wise God our Savior, be glory and majesty, dominion and power, both now and ever." Jude 24, 25.

. . . .

Explain the term, *benediction.*

Lesson XLIV

II Peter

It is apparent that II Peter is closely related to the Epistle of Jude. The purpose of this epistle, like that of Jude, is to combat certain false teachings. The warnings are repeated with a new emphasis that indicates that the heresy had grown worse since the writing of Jude. Early authorities ascribe the authorship of the book to Peter, and think that he wrote it shortly before his death. The book itself states that Peter is its author (1:1; 2:1).

I. Salutation (1:1-2)

II. Exhortation to steadfastness (1:3-11)

III. Divine authority of Christian tradition (1:12-21)

IV. Warnings against the false teachers (2:1-3:4)

V. Certainty of Christ's return in judgment (3:5-13)

VI. Final exhortation to righteous living (3:14-18)

Questions—Lesson XLIV.

1. What virtues are Christians exhorted to add to their faith? (1:5-8)
2. What is the source of all true prophecy? (1:21)

3. What is said about God's keeping his promises? (3:9)
4. What is the author's final exhortation to Christians? (3:18)

Memorize:
What virtues are Christians exhorted to add to their faith? "Giving all diligence, add to your faith virtue; and to virtue knowledge; And to knowledge temperance; and to temperance patience; and to patience godliness; And to godliness brotherly kindness; and to brotherly kindness charity. For if these things be in you, and abound, they make you that ye shall neither be barren nor unfruitful in the knowledge of our Lord Jesus Christ." II Peter 1:5-8.

Lesson XLV

Revelation

The Book of Revelation is an Apocalyptic writing; i.e., it is a revelation. Daniel is the Old Testament book of this type. Revelation was written by John who was a prisoner on the Isle of Patmos. It is usually considered that he was John the beloved disciple. It is possible that he was John of Ephesus who was an influential figure in the churches of Asia Minor. The writer seems to be familiar with the people to whom he is writing—the Churches of Asia Minor: Ephesus, Smyrna, Pergamum, Thyatira, Sardis, Philadelphia, and Laodicea. All of these Churches are near Ephesus where Paul spent three years on his third missionary journey.

Revelation was written during a period of persecution, in the latter years of the reign of the Roman Emperor Domitian (81-96 A.D.). The date of the book should be placed around A.D. 93-95. Domitian set up his image in the provinces to be worshipped. To worship the image of the emperor was to deny the Christian faith. Because the Christians would not comply with the laws set down by Rome, they came under persecution. Revelation was written to the Christians of Asia Minor to encourage them during the persecution. The author places emphasis upon the glorious day that is coming for those who remain faithful. This book cannot be rightly interpreted except in the light of the practical situations that were facing the Christians of that particular period of history.

Revelation has three natural divisions:

1. Introduction: Letters to the Seven Churches. Chapters 1-3.
2. The Judgments on Earth. Chapters 4-18.
3. The Day of Triumph. Chapters 19-22.

Note: Each of the above divisions should be sub-divided into smaller sections; but for the practical purposes of this course it is believed advisable to leave the outline in the larger divisions and let teachers who find time to do so make a more detailed outline.

Questions—Lesson XLV.

1. Name and locate the seven churches to whom the messages are sent.
2. Note three series of judgments:
   a. The opening of the seven seals, 6:1-8:1.
   b. The sounding of the seven trumpets, 8:2-10:7.
   c. The emptying of the seven bowls, 15:1-20:3.
3. Give your interpretation of the following passages: 2:10 (last part); 3:20; 22:14, 17.

Memorize:

A promise to the faithful: "Be thou faithful unto death and I will give thee a crown of life." Revelation 2:10.

Quotations for careful study:

"Blessed are they that do His commandments, that they may have right to the tree of life, and may enter in through the gates into the city." Revelation 22:14.

. . . .

Explain the following terms: *apocalypse, almighty,* and *oracles.*

APPENDIX

SELECTED REFERENCES

ARCHAEOLOGY

Barton, Geo. A. *Archaeology of the Bible.* Am. S. S. Union, 1933. (Good) $3.50.

Kinnemon, J. O. *Diggers for Facts.* Destiny Pub. Co., 1941. (New) $2.50.

Marston, Sir Chas. *New Bible Evidence.* Revell, 1933. $2.00.

Muir, J. C. *His Truth Endureth.* National Pub. Co., 1937. (Old Test.) $2.50.

Muir, J. C. *The Spade and the Scriptures.* Broadman Press. (A study course on *His Truth Endureth*) (Brief, helpful) $.60.

Muir, J. C. *How Firm a Foundation.* National Pub. Co., 1941 (new) $2.50.

Price, Ira. *The Monuments of the Old Testament.* Judson Press, 1924. $2.50.

Prescott, W. W. *The Spade and the Bible.* Revell. $2.00.

Rimmer, Harry. *Dead Men Tell Tales.* Eerdman Pub. Co., 1939. (Good) $2.50.

ATLAS

Hurlburt, J. L. *Bible Atlas.* Rand McNally, 1938. (Excellent) $3.50.

BACKGROUNDS

Adams, J. McKee. *Biblical Backgrounds.* Broadman Press, 1934. (Good) $3.75.

Baike, Jas. *Lands and Peoples of the Bible.* Macmillan. $1.75.

Harrell, C. J. *The Bible: Its Origin and Growth.* Cokesbury, 1926. $1.00.

Morton, H. V. *Through the Land of Bible.* Dodd Mead. $1.79.
Soares, Theo. G. *The Origins of the Bible.* Harpers, 1941. (New) $2.50.

COMMENTARY

Brown, Lewis. *Graphic Bible Commentary.* Macmillan. (From Gen. to Rev. Animated charts and maps). $1.00.

Dummelow, J. R. *One Volume Bible Commentary.* Macmillan, 1923. (Good) $3.00.

Eislen-Lewis-Downey. *Abingdon Bible Commentary.* Abingdon Press, 1929. (One of the best single volume commentaries.) $5.00.

Halley, Henry H. *Pocket Bible Handbook.* Published by author. 1944. $2.00.

Irwin, C. H. *The International Bible Commentary.* Winston, 1928. (Brief) $2.50.

Tidwell, J. B. *The Bible Book by Book.* Eerdman Pub. Co., (Practical). $1.75.

[81]

CONCORDANCE

Cruden, Alexander. *A Complete Concordance.* Winston (Standard). $2.50.

Joy, Chas. R. *Harper's Topical Concordance.* Harper, 1940 (New). $3.95.

DICTIONARY

Davis, John B. *Bible Dictionary.* Westminister, 1944. $3.50.

Hastings, Jas. *Dictionary of the Bible.* Scribners, 1937. (Standard) $7.00.

Peloubet. *Bible Dictionary.* Winston, 1925. (Good) $2.50.

Smith, Wm. *Bible Dictionary.* Winston, 1938. (Good) $2.00.

Zenos, Jacobus, and Lane. *New Standard Bible Dictionary.* Funk & Wagnalls, 1936. $7.50.

HARMONY

Burton-Goodspeed. *A Harmony of the Synthetic Gospels.* Scribners. $2.00.

Kerr, John H. *Harmony of the Gospels.* Revell, 1924. $1.25.

Robertson, A. T. *A Harmony of the Gospels.* Harper, 1922. (Excellent). $2.50.

GENERAL

Butterick, Geo. A. *Parables of Jesus.* Harper. $1.50.

Carter, Thomas. *Life and Letters of Paul.* Cokesbury, 1931. $1.00.

Dalton, T. M. and Martin, W. C. *Comprehensive Bible Study Course.* Mathis, Van Nort, 1940. $1.50.

Egermieres, Elsie E. *The Story of the Bible.* Warner Press, 1939 (Good). $2.50.

Erdman, Charles. *The Gospel of Matthew.* The Westminister Press. $1.00. (By the same author, separate volumes on Mark, Luke, John, Acts, Pastoral Letters, etc. Complete set of 17 volumes for $15.00. A most convenient and authoritative commentary on the New Testament. Separate volumes, $1.00 each.)

Goodspeed, Edgar J. *The Story of the New Testament.* Univ. of Chicago Press. $1.00.

Gray, J. M. *Synthetic Bible Stories.* Revell. $2.25.

Hurlburt, J. L. *The Story of the Bible.* Winston. (Excellent) $2.50.

Josephus, Flavius. *Life and Works.* Revell. $3.00.

Luccock, Halford E. *The Acts of the Apostles,* Vol. I. Willet-Clark. $1.50.

Luccock, Halford E. *The Acts of the Apostles,* Vol. II. Willet-Clark. $1.50. (Vol. I published in 1938; Vol. II, 1939.)

Martin, Hugh. *The Parables of the Gospel.* Abingdon, 1937. (Good) $2.00.

Morgan, G. Campbell. *The Acts of the Apostles.* Revell. $3.75.

Morton, H. V. *In the Steps of the Master* Dodd, Mead, 1939. $3.50.

Morton, H. V. *In the Steps of Paul.* Dodd, Mead, 1937. $3.50.

Stalker, Jas. *Life of Christ.* Revell. $1.25.

Stalker, Jas. *Life of Paul.* Revell. $1.25.

THE LAND AND THE BOOK*

By WILLIAM NEHEMIAH WIGGINS,
*For twenty-five years General Superintendent
of Texas Sunday School Association*

Someone said, "The Land is the fifth Gospel." It is absolutely impossible to understand fully the meaning of the language used in the Bible without having a comprehensive knowledge of the geography of the land and the customs and manners of the people which prevailed when the Bible was written.

The following brief paragraphs have been compiled with the hope that they may be helpful to teachers of Bible classes, particularly to the less experienced teacher. We have quoted very liberally from "The Teaching Values of the Old Testament," by Drs. W. W. Moore and Edward Mack, which has been fully verified by the writer, in almost every detail, while he personally visited and studied the land in connection with the World Sunday School Convention at Jerusalem in 1904.

The Palestinian Atmosphere of the Bible. "Like other books the Bible has had a home, a birthplace; but beyond all other examples, this birthplace has given color and form to its language." The phraseology and imagery of the Bible reflect in a remarkable degree the character of the country in which it was written and the customs of the people among whom it arose. We must learn the land and the life of ancient Israel if we would apprehend the whole setting of revealed truth and appreciate the force of a multitude of metaphors and allusions which otherwise would have no meaning.

The Land and the Redemptive Purpose of God. Not only is it is essential to study Palestine for an intelligent appreciation of Biblical forms and statements of surface facts of Biblical history, but it is vital to a full understanding of the inner relations of those facts to each other as parts of one divine purpose and stages in one divine revelation, unfolded gradually through hundreds of years and culminating in a universal religion.

The Land of Promise was preconfigured to its history. It was through the characteristics of the country that God effected fufillment of the promise to Abraham, that in his

---

NOTE: To Drs. W. W. Moore and Edward Mack in *Teaching Values of Old Testament,* we are indebted for much of the descriptions contained in this outline on "The Land and the Book." The present article is an abridgment of an earlier treatment prepared by Mr. Wiggins.

seed should all the nations of the earth be blessed. By its location and structure it was adapted, as no other country on earth, to God's purpose of preparing a pure religion through centuries of separation and then of publishing that religion to the whole world. For the accomplishment of these ends, three things seemed necessary:

1. A single nation had to be chosen as the special depository of divine truth. This nation had to be *separated* from all other nations in order that this truth might be preserved and developed in its purity. This isolation of Israel was secured by natural barriers of desert, river, sea, and mountain.

2. This nation had to be set in the *center* of the world so that when "the fullness of time was come," the saving truth which it possessed might be easily proclaimed to all mankind. Palestine was central. It was the focal point of the ancient world. It commanded access to three great continents—Europe, Asia, and Africa. Palestine stood in the midst of the nations of antiquity. It was therefore fitted, as no other land was, to be the radiating center of a universal religion.

3. The book which contained this revelation had to be a *universal* book. It could not be local or sectional. It must possess such a range of imagery and style as would make it easily understood by men of every race in every land. The Record of the Truth thus prepared had to be such as would fit it for world-wide dissemination. It must speak to the universal heart of man by its essential truth. It must have characteristics of form adapted to the ready understanding of men of all lands.

The Structure of Palestine. Palestine could not have been a mere accident in God's creation. The structure of Palestine preeminently fitted it to produce such a book as the Bible. It is a very small country, ranging from 25 to 75 miles in width, and about 140 miles in length. Yet in this small strip we have extraordinary differences of elevation and climate, with snow on Mount Hermon and torrid heat at Jericho. Mount Hermon has an elevation of 9,200 feet above the Mediterranean, and the Dead Sea is 1,292 feet below the Mediterranean. This great variation in topography accounts for the amazing variety of animal and vegetable life, representing widely separated zones and making it a sort of epitome of the whole earth. "Accordingly, the illustrations drawn from nature, with which the Bible abounds, are suited to all climes and understood by all men."

The Land's Natural Divisions. Palestine consists of four strips of territory, running parallel to each other north and south, with two elevations and two depressions alternating. A narrow plain skirts the Mediterranean. Next to this is a tumbled and broken ridge rising to an altitude of 3,000 feet.

Then comes the extraordinary depressions through which flows the River Jordan; and after this, the elevated tablelands lying between the Jordan and the Eastern Desert. *The Mediterranean Plain a Highway.* This narrow Mediterranean plain, level or gently undulating, open at both ends, was the bridge between Asia and Africa. It was traversed by highways along which the caravans and armies of two continents passed to and fro. Here we find the real contribution of Israel to history. By the Trunk Road through this plain, the Philistines came up to the overthrow of Saul at Mount Gilboa. Along this road the Jews saw the armies of Tiglah-Pileser, Shalmaneser, Saragon, Sennacherib, Pharaoh-Necho, and Nebuchadnezzar pass. It was the world's highway.

The most striking feature of the coast line is that it had no good harbor. The Hebrews had no word for harbor because they had no need for the name. To them the sea was a barrier and not a highway. That long line of sand, unbroken by any deep indentation, cut Israel off almost entirely from water communication with the western world. *Seclusion* is the dominant note in the *Old Testament*. *Expansion* is the dominant note in the *New Testament*. When God's time came He raised a man, who was unconsciously His instrument for the breaking of a gateway through which the Gospel should go forth to the west. Herod the Great, for the first time in history, built a real harbor for Palestine at Caesarea. Thence the Great Apostle to the Gentiles went forth with the Gospel to the Western World.

The Plain of Esdraelon a Highway and Battlefield. Esdraelon is the great triangular plain which breaks the continuity of the Central Ridge and affords clear passage from the coast to the Jordan. Through this plain the marauding Bedouin passed from the East. The armies of the great empires passed this way; hence, the plain's history as a great battlefield. Isaiah 19:23.

Samaria Easy of Acess. The gentle ridges on the west offer an easy access from the coast. Interspersed among the mountains in the center are plains, meadows, and spacious vales; hence the land was easy for chariots. "All the long drives of the Old Testament are in Samaria." One result was frequent invasions. Its connection with Eastern Palestine has existed from the earliest times to the present day. The easy access, the easy passes, and numerous fords of the Jordan here, are in sharp contrast with the separation of Judea from the East, because of the steep chasm and the few and dangerous fords farther south. Through the accessibility of Samaria, the "surrounding paganism poured into her ample life." Samaria suffered many changes of rulers. The Northern Kingdom had nine dynasties. The Southern Kingdom had only one dynasty. The Northern Kingdom fell more than a hundred years before the Southern. In short, as Smith says, Samaria was more forward to attract than Judea, but less able to retain.

Spiritual Supremacy of Judea. Judea was the heart of the Land of Palestine, the seat of Israel's one enduring dynasty, the site of her Temple, and the platform of all her chief prophets. Isolated, unattractive, provincial, conservative, she held the world off the longest. Study carefully the borders and bulwarks of this stony plateau. The most accessible frontier was on the north, and here accordingly many battles were fought. Judea was a stronghold, not impregnable, but very difficult to take. (It is interesting to study the direction from which General Allenby of the Allies came to capture Jerusalem during the World War.) Outstanding features of the province are its pastoral character, says Smith, and its vine culture, and its natural unfitness for the growth of a large city. Aloof, waterless, on the road to nowhere, yet here arose the city which has taught the world civil justice, has given through the Cross eternal salvation, and has given her name to the ideal city hoped for—the New Jerusalem.

The Jordan Valley a Barrier. The lower Jordan is thought of as a border and a barrier. The name is nearly always governed by a preposition, "unto," "over," "across." A jungle along its bank, it is a symbol of trouble and danger. Study the miraculous way Israel crossed the Jordan here.

The Eastern Range. The Eastern Highlands are generally well-watered and fertile; but being separated from the body of the nation by the gorge of the Jordan, had comparatively small influence on the course of history.

The Manners and Customs of the People. The imagery of scripture, since it is drawn from natural scenery, is consequently readily understood in all parts of the world. Not so with the customs and manners of the people. The Old Testament is an Oriental book, as is the New very largely. The life the Bible describes belongs to the East and is widely different from the life in the West. Nearly every feature of it is foreign to our experience, and it undergoes very little change from age to age.

The past decade has been marked by capitalists and settlers

from without, coming in and introducing many modern features, such as railroads, telegraph lines, printing presses, automobiles, airplanes, hotels, etc. Still all these have to this day had very little or practically no effect on the patriarchal usages of the body of the people.

LANGUAGE AND MANUSCRIPTS OF THE BIBLE*

By Dr. Glenn L. Sneed,
Former Pastor of Trinity Presbyterian Church, Dallas.

1. *Name.* The name Bible is derived from the Greek word *Biblos*, meaning "Book" or "The Book." The term *biblos* is itself said to be derived from *byblos*, the inner bark of the papyrus reed on which early writings were inscribed. Well may the Bible be called "the Book." It is the best seller in all of the greatest book stores in the world and is the most widely quoted book in the world's best literature.

2. *Language.* Most of the Old Testament is written in the Hebrew language. A number of small portions (Jeremiah 10:11; Daniel 2:4-7:28; Ezra 4:8-6:18, 7:12-26) and a few scattered words are written in a tongue called "Aramaic," formerly known as "Chaldee." For centuries Aramaic was the language of the people north of Palestine (northern Syria, western Mesopotamia, and southeastern Asia Minor). The New Testament was written not in classical Greek, nor even in the literary Greek of New Testament times, but in the common Greek language of everyday life.

3. *Hand writing.* The earliest copies that we have of the Bible are written in uncial letters; that is, capital letters. There were no spaces between the words and in the case of the Hebrew the vowels had to be supplied by the reader. The later translations were written in the cursive or running hand.

4. *Original Manuscripts.* Everything written on perishable material such as papyrus and skin is always in great danger of being lost or destroyed. Men of old realized this fact and in order to preserve the sacred writings, and at the same time give copies to more people, they laboriously transcribed them again and again. There were numerous copies other than the original in existence. Consequently from these

---

*Revised by Reverend Seaborn Kiker, Pastor of the Irwindell Methodist Church, Dallas, Texas.

copies of the original manuscripts others were made. Had it not been for this, the Bible would not be known to us; for not a single copy of an original manuscript is known to exist today.

5. *Lost Writings.* It is also true that some of the earlier "books" or writings referred to in the Bible have been lost, as is seen from the following quotations: "The Book of the Wars of Jehovah" (Numbers 21:14) ; "The Book of Jasher" (Joshua 10:13 and II Samuel 1:18; "The Book of Iddo the Seer" (II Chronicles 12:15) ; "The Book of Nathan" (I Chronicles 29:29) ; and "The Book of Gad" (I Chronicles 29:29).

6. *Manuscript and Versions.* (a. The Septuagint—pronounced sep'-tu-a-gint.) Long before the time of Christ there was a great settlement of Jews in Alexandria, Egypt. Seventy Jewish scholars translated the sacred Scriptures into the Hellenistic Greek, the universal language of their day. This translation, known as the *Septuagint,* was used in the synagogues at the time of Christ. (b. Three Famous MSS.) According to the claim of scholars, copies out of the original languages are known as manuscripts, and translated into other languages are called versions. We have in existence today three very famous MSS: (1) The Vatican, the earliest, has lain in the Vatican at Rome for something like 500 years. (2) The Cinaitic, which was discovered by Dr. Tischendorf in St. Catherine's Monastery at Mt. Sinai. This is now in the British Museum, London. The story of the discovery and the recovery of this very ancient manuscript is as interesting as a novel. (3) The Alexandrian. This manuscript was presented to Charles I by Cyril Lucar of Constantinople, 1628 A.D. It arrived in London seventeen years too late to be used in the making of the King James Version of the Bible. This manuscript is now kept in the British Museum. It is worthy of note that these three manuscripts are in the possession of the Roman Catholic Church and the Protestant Church. It is also worthy of note that none of these was available when the King James Version was written, but facsimile copies of these were in possession of those scholars who gave us the American Standard Version and other revised versions.

Among the many versions in which the Bible has been translated, one of the most famous is the Latin Vulgate, which was translated by the great Latin scholar, Jerome. This Latin Vulgate is practically the Bible of the Roman Catholic Church today. There are many other versions, such as the Syraic scriptures, the Egyptian, the Ethiopic, and Armenian. The later translations are those of Wycliffe, Tyndale, Coverdale,

The Great Bible, The Geneva Bible, and our authorized Bible and the American Revised, etc. In addition to these splendid versions, we have the modern translation by individual scholars, such as the Moffatt and Goodspeed translations. Their main attempt is to translate the Bible into modern thought and language.

LITERARY CHARACTERISTICS OF THE BIBLE

By Dr. Umphrey Lee,
President of Southern Methodist University, Dallas.

In our study of the Bible we must not neglect a consideration of its literary character. The English Bible has contributed more phrases to our common language, has stiumlated the thinking of more of our writers, and has been the delight of more readers than any other book in our language. An appreciation of the different kinds of literature contained in this one volume, and the ability to read with pleasure its love-songs, narratives, religious poetry, and letters should be a part of every educated man's acquirement. In this short essay, there will be pointed out only (1) the character of the language, (2) the nature of the poetry, and (3) the general literary types of the Bible.

1. *Language.* For our purpose the Bible is an English book; although the Old Testament was originally written almost altogether in Hebrew and the New Testament in Greek, while the two have been translated into almost every known language and dialect. Yet the Bible which most students will read is an English book. Because of this the language and style of the Bible are essentially the same throughout. Fortunately, our King James Version, the one most commonly used, was translated in a time, the so-called Elizabethan Age, when the English language was yet simple and concrete, in every way fitted to translate the Hebrew and Greek of the Bible.

Ancient Hebrew was a language with few words for abstract ideas; most Hebrew words had "a physical significa-tion." A great French scholar illustrated this characteristic of Hebrew by calling attention to the way the Old Testament avoids the use of such comparatively simple abstractions as "discouragement," "despair," "pride." *Discouragement* and *despair* are expressed by the melting of the heart. *Pride* is portrayed by the holding high of the head, with the figure straight and stiff. *Patience* is a long breathing, *impatience* short breathing, *desire* is thirst or paleness. (Cf. Psalms 22:7, 14, 24.)

In the same way, the Greek language in which the New Testament was written was not the involved Greek of the classics, but a simple, popular tongue, spoken throughout the Mediterranean world in the centuries immediately preceding and succeeding the Christian era. If you read a few verses from John's Gospel, you will see the simplest form of this language: there are few dependent clauses, and the connectives are usually *and, but, for,* etc.

The student who would appreciate the peculiar fitness of Elizabethan English for the translation of the Bible should read the Dedicatory Letter to King James written by the translators in 1611, which is even yet printed in some copies of that version. Here they will find the rich, colorful phrases which we associate with Hebrew poetry and the concrete words which are characteristic both of the Bible and of Shakespeare.[1]

2. *Poetry.* In the vivid vocabulary of the Hebrew and Greek writers, the Bible contains a great deal of poetry. Therefore one who would read the Bible with pleasure must know how to distinguish prose from poetry and must learn to read the poetry with appreciation. English poetry is usually characterized by meter and rhyme, and even "free verse" is printed in a peculiar way. But the Hebrew poetry has neither rhyme nor meter (speaking generally), and in the older versions of the English Bible poetry and prose are printed alike. First, then, let us ask: What is the essential characteristic of Hebrew poetry?

If we turn to the Psalms, we can study the various ways in which the Hebrews varied their fundamental poetic principle.

> The heavens declare the glory of God;
> And the firmament sheweth his handiwork. (Psalms 19:1)

Here is the simplest form of Hebrew poetry, in which the second line of a couplet repeats the sense of the first line but in different words. Hebrew poetry consists in a "balance of

---

[1]On this and other matters relating to the Bible as English literature, the student should consult J. H. Gardiner, *The Bible as English Literature.* New York, 1916.

thought contained in the words rather than in the balance of the number of syllables." This balance is called "parallelism."

Sometimes the second line adds to the thought of the first:

O clap your hands, all ye people;
Shout unto God with voice of triumph. (Psalms 47:1)

Again, the second line will introduce a thought opposite to that set forth in the first:

For the Lord knoweth the way of the righteous:
But the way of the ungodly shall perish. (Psalms 1:6.)

Occasionally each line will develop something suggested by the preceding, thus building up the thought in a "stair-case" or "spiral" fashion, as in the following example:

I will lift up mine eyes unto the hills,
From whence cometh my help;
My help cometh from the Lord,
Which made heaven and earth. (Psalms 121:1.)

3. *Literary Types.* To understand and read with pleasure the Bible one should recognize the *different types of literature* which are found in it. There are *narratives* such as the stories of Joseph (Genesis 37, 39-46), and of David (I and II Samuel). There are *lyrics* such as the Psalms and other short poems scattered through the historical and prophetic books. The Book of Job is a *dramatic poem,* in which different characters are introduced, who express their views in long poetic speeches. Much of the Old Testament is taken up by books which we call *prophetic.* These—Amos, Hosea, Micah, Isaiah, Jeremiah, etc.—are deliverances by the "prophets" on religious, moral, and political conditions of their times, with predictions of the course of events. under certain moral conditions. In the New Testament, we have the *Gospels,* accounts of the Life and Teachings of Jesus, and the *Letters* (usually called Epistles) mainly written by Paul. The latter are real letters with salutations and formal endings such as were common in that day.

The student who seeks an appreciation of the literary character of the Bible should study one or two of the Psalms for examples of parallelism. He should glance through some modern edition of the Bible which prints the poetical section in the form of poetry, in order that he may see how much of the Bible is poetical. To distinguish the different types of literature in the Bible, the student should read some narratives; as the story of Joseph, the Prophecy of Amos, at least a part of the Book of Job, the Gospel according to Mark, and the Epistle of Philemon.

REVIEW QUESTIONS

1. How long has Jesus existed?
2. Why is an understanding of the Old Testament necessary to a study of the New Testament?
3. What was the last revelation from God before Christ came?
4. What was the first inspired writing after Christ came?
5. How much time elapsed between the writing of Malachi and Mark?
6. In what ways were world conditions suitable for the coming of Christ?
7. What is peculiarly significant about the birth of Jesus? Explain the significance of the related incidents.
8. What do we know about the childhood of Jesus?
9. What do we know about the next eighteen years of His life?
10. Explain how the ministry of John the Baptist helped to prepare for the beginning of Christ's ministry.
11. Why did Jesus request baptism of John?
12. How were the temptations of Jesus a vital part of the preparation for His ministry?
13. What new teaching did Jesus give Nicodemus?
14. Explain the significance of the rejection of Jesus at Nazareth.
15. What characterizes the Great Galilean Ministry of Jesus?
16. What caused the popularity of Jesus to mount so high in the Galilean Ministry? What climaxed this popularity with many of His followers?
17. Why may the Sermon on the Mount be considered as a basis of Christian living?
18. What did Jesus say one should seek first?
19. According to Jesus, on what do wise people build their life?
20. What fundamental truth had Jesus established among His disciples, as was evidenced by Peter's confession?
21. What great prophecy did Jesus make following Peter's confession?
22. At the transfiguration of Jesus, how did God emphasize the fact that Jesus was the authority of the New Testament?

23. What methods did Jesus employ in His teaching? Where did He teach?
24. Among what class of people was Jesus popular? Among what classes was he unpopular? Why?
25. Was Jesus satisfied to be recognized as a prophet?
26. Who according to Jesus will be greatest in the kingdom of heaven?
27. What did Jesus teach concerning forgiveness?
28. How did Jesus teach reverence for places of worship?
29. Why did Jesus need to go away?
30. What assurance do we have that Jesus will come again?
31. How did Jesus comfort His disciples in His departing message?
32. What was the reaction of the disciples after the arrest and crucifixion of Jesus?
33. What convinced the disciples that Jesus had really risen?
34. What was the significance of the raising of Lazarus from the dead?
35. Why did Jesus perform miracles? Name five miracles performed by Him?
36. What was the purpose of the writing of the Gospels?
37. By what plan did Christ expect His Gospel to be promulgated?
38. Was the birth, life, death and resurrection of Jesus according to prophecy?
39. Acts is the continuation of what writing?
40. What are the two natural divisions of Acts?
41. Who is the outstanding character in each division?
42. Through whom was the Gospel first given to the Gentiles?
43. Who was the outstanding missionary to the Gentiles?
44. What great contribution did Paul make to Christianity?
45. What was the chief purpose of Paul's journeys?
46. Contrast the early life of Paul with his later life.
47. What do the letters in the New Testament mean to us today?
48. What fundamental facts do we need to know about any book in the Bible in order to "rightly divide the word of truth"?
49. Describe the nature of the writings in Revelation.
50. Were all the writings of the New Testament inspired? (II Tim. 3:16, 17; II Peter 1:20, 21)

QUOTATIONS FOR CAREFUL STUDY
(For Review Purposes)

Lesson I.

1. First mention of Christ: "And God said, 'Let us make man in our image, after our likeness.'" Genesis 1:26.

2. First promise concerning Christ: "And will put enmity between thee and the woman, and between thy seed and her seed; it shall bruise thy head, and thou shalt bruise his heel." Genesis 3:15.

3. Isaiah's prophecy about Christ: "He was numbered with the transgressors; and He bare the sin of many, and made intercession for the transgressors." Isaiah 53:12.

4. "Glory to God in the highest, and on earth peace, good will toward men." Luke 2:14.

Lesson II.

5. John announces his office: "I am the voice of one crying in the wilderness, 'Make straight the way of the Lord, as said the prophet Esaias.'" John 1:23.

6. John's testimony concerning Jesus: "The latchet of whose shoes I am not worthy to unloose." Mark 1:7.

7. "Know ye not that I must be about my Father's business?" Luke 2:49.

Lesson III.

8. Necessity of a new birth: "Marvel not that I say unto thee, thou must be born again." John 3:7.

9. "God is a spirit; and they that worship Him must worship Him in spirit and in truth." John 4:24.

10. Doing the Father's will: "My meat is to do the will of Him that sent me, and to finish His work." John 4:34.

Lesson IV.

11. Jesus has power to forgive sin: "The Son of Man hath power on earth to forgive sins." Matthew 9:6.

Lesson V.

12. A metaphor Jesus used to show the influence of his followers: "Ye are the salt of the earth." Matthew 5:13.

13. A metaphor Jesus used to show the influence of his followers: "Ye are the light of the world." Matthew 5:16.

14. "For where your treasure is, there will your heart be also." Matthew 6:21.

15. "Judge not, that ye be not judged." Matthew 7:1.

16. "By their fruits ye shall know them." Matthew 7:20.

17. "For He taught them as one having authority, and not as the scribes." Matthew 7:49.

Lesson VI.

18. "Art thou He that should come, or look we for another?" Luke 7:19.

19. Christ's tribute to John the Baptist: "Among those that are born of women there hath not risen a greater than John the Baptist." Matthew 11:11.

20. Jesus proclaims John the Baptist as His forerunner: "This is He of whom it is written, 'Behold I send my messenger before thy face, which shall prepare thy way before thee.'" Luke 7:27.

Lesson VII.

21. "A prophet is not without honor, save in his own country, and in his own house." Matthew 13:57.

22. "I am the bread of life." John 6:35.

23. "It is I; be not afraid." John 6:20.

Lesson VIII.

24. "Thou art the Christ, the Son of the living God." Matthew 16:16.

25. "Master, it is good for us to be here." Mark 9:5.

26. What one must do in order to follow Chirst: "If any man come after me, let him deny himself, and take up his cross daily, and follow me." Luke 9:23.

Lesson IX.

27. "I am the Light of the world." John 8:12.

28. "I am the good shepherd, and know my sheep, and am known of mine." John 10:14.

Lesson X.

29. "The life is more than meat, and the body is more than raiment." Luke 12:23.

Lesson XII.

30. "God be merciful to me a sinner." Luke 18:13.

31. "Suffer little children, and forbid them not, to come unto me: for of such is the kingdom of heaven." Matthew 19:14.

Lesson XIII.

32. "Render unto Caesar the things which are Caesar's; and unto God the things that are God's." Matthew 22:21.

Lesson XIV.

33. "Well done, good and faithful servant; thou hast been faithful over a few things: enter thou into the joy of the Lord." Matthew 25:23.

34. "For I was an hungered, and ye gave me meat: I was thirsty and ye gave me drink: I was a stranger and ye took me in:

"Naked and ye clothed me: I was sick, and ye visited me: I was in prison and ye came unto me." Matthew 25:35, 36.

Lesson XV.

35. "This do in remembrance of me." Luke 22:19.

36. "Herein is my Father glorified, that ye bear much fruit: so shall ye be my disciples." John 15:8.

Lesson XVI.

37. "They parted my garments among them, and upon my vesture did they cast lots." Matthew 27:35.

38. "Certainly this was a righteous man." Luke 23:47.

Lesson XVII.

39. "Did not our heart burn within us, while He talked with us by the way, and while He opened to us the Scriptures?" Luke 24:32.

40. "He is not here, but is risen." Luke 24:6.

Lesson XVIII.

41. "And when the day of Pentecost was fully come, they were all with one accord in one place." Acts 2:1.

42. The growth of the Church: "The Lord added to the Church daily such as should be saved." Acts 2:47.

43. "Lord, lay not this sin to their charge." Acts 7:60.

Lesson XIX.

44. New name for the disciples: "And the disciples were called Christians first at Antioch." Acts 11:26.

Lesson XX.

45. "God made choice among us, that the Gentiles by my mouth should hear the word of the gospel and believe." Acts 15:17.

Lesson XXII.

46. "It is more blessed to give than to receive." Acts 20:35.

Lesson XXIII.

47. "I would to God, that not only thou, but also all that hear me this day, were both almost, and altogether such as I am, except these bonds." Acts 26:29.

Lesson XXVII.

48. "Eye hath not seen, nor ear heard, neither have entered into the heart of man, the things which God hath prepared for them that love Him." I Corinthians 2:9.

49. "But take heed lest by any means this liberty of yours become a stumbling block to them that are weak." I Corinthians 8:9.

Lesson XXVIII.

50. The basis of Christian giving: "Upon the first day of the week let every one of you lay by him in store, as God hath prospered him." II Corinthian 16:2.

51. The basis for Christian reward: "He which soweth sparingly shall reap also sparingly; and he which soweth bountifully shall reap also bountifully." II Corinthians 9:6.

Lesson XXIX.

52. "For I am not ashamed of the gospel of Christ; for it is the power of God unto salvation to every one that believeth; to the Jew first, and also to the Greek." Romans 1:16.

53. "The powers that be are ordained of God." Romans 13:1.

54. What fulfills the law? "Owe no man anything, but to love one another." Romans 13:8.

Lesson XXX.

55. Where should Christians center their affections? "Set your affections on things above, not on things on the earth." Colossians 3:2.

Lesson XXXIII.

56. How may one resist temptation? "Put on the whole armor of God that ye may be able to stand against the wiles of the devil." Ephesians 6:11.

57. "Children, obey your parents in the Lord: for this is right. Honor thy father and mother; which is the first commandment with promise." Ephesians 6:1-2.

Lesson XXXVI.

58. "Every good gift and every perfect gift is from above, and cometh down from the Father of lights." James 1:17. "Resist the devil and he will flee from you." James 4:7.

Lesson XXXVII.

59. "Let no man despise thy youth; but be thou an example of the believers, in word, in conversation, in charity, in spirit, in faith, in purity." I Timothy 4:12.

Lesson XL.

60. "We love Him because He first loved us." I John 4:19.

Lesson XLIII.

61. "Now unto Him that is able to keep you from falling, and to present you faultless before the presence of His glory with exceeding joy,

"To the only wise God our Savior, be glory and majesty, dominion and power, both now and ever." Jude 24, 25.

Lesson XLV.

62. "Blessed are they that do His commandments, that they may have right to the tree of life, and may enter in through the gates into the city." Revelation 22:14.

REQUIRED MEMORY VERSES
(For Review Purposes)

(Pupils should be able to reproduce from memory each of the following quotations when given the accompanying lead, the book, chapter, and verse reference.)

Lesson I.

1. The pre-existence of Christ

"In the beginning was the Word, and the Word was with God, and the Word was God . . . All things were made by him; and without him was not anything made that was made . . . And the Word was made flesh, and dwelt among us, (and we beheld his glory, the glory as of the only begotten of the Father,) full of grace and truth." John 1:1, 3, 14.

Lesson II.

2. Jesus to the devil in the wilderness

"It is written, Man shall not live by bread alone, but by every word that proceedeth out of the mouth of God . . . It is written again, Thou shalt not tempt the Lord thy God . . . Get thee hence, Satan: for it is written, Thou shalt worship the Lord thy God, and him only shalt thou serve." Matthew 4:4, 7, 10.

Lesson III.

3. The purpose of Christ's coming

"For God so loved the world that he gave his only begotten Son, that whosoever believeth in him should not perish, but have eternal life." John 3:16.

Lesson IV.

4. Jesus reprimands the Pharisees for their ignorance of the scriptures

"Search the scriptures; for in them ye think ye have eternal life: and they are they which testify of me." John 5:39

Lesson V.

5. Beautitudes

"Blessed are the poor in spirit: for theirs is the kingdom of heaven.

"Blessed are they that mourn: for they shall be comforted.

"Blessed are the meek: for they shall inherit the earth.

"Blessed are they which do hunger and thirst after righteousness: for they shall be filled.

"Blessed are the merciful: for they shall obtain mercy.

"Blessed are the pure in heart: for they shall see God.

"Blessed are the peacemakers: for they shall be called the children of God.

"Blessed are they which are persecuted for righteousness' sake: for theirs is the kingdom of heaven.

"Blessed are ye, when men shall revile you, and persecute you, and shall say all manner of evil against you falsely, for my sake.

"Rejoice and be exceeding glad: for great is your reward in heaven: for so persecuted they the prophets which were before you." Matthew 5:3-12.

6. The Lord's Prayer

"Our Father which art in heaven, Hallowed be thy name.

"Thy kingdom come. Thy will be done in earth, as it is in heaven.

"Give us this day our daily bread.

"And forgive us our debts, as we forgive our debtors.

"And lead us not into temptation, but deliver us from evil:

"For thine is the kingdom, and the power, and the glory, forever. Amen." Matthew 6:9-13.

7. The Golden Rule

"Therefore all things whatsoever ye would that men should do to you, do ye even so to them: for this is the law and the prophets." Matthew 7:12.

8. What shall we seek above all else?

"But seek ye first the kingdom of God, and his righteousness; and all these things shall be added unto you." Matthew 6:33.

9. The three-fold promise of prayer

"Ask, and it shall be given you; seek, and ye shall find; knock, and it shall be opened unto you." Matthew 7:7.

Lesson VI.

10a. "Lord, to whom shall we go? Thou hast the words of eternal life." John 6:68.

10b. The invitation of Jesus

"Come unto me, all ye that labor and are heavy laden, and I will give you rest. Take my yoke upon you, and learn of me; for I am meek and lowly in heart: and ye shall find rest unto your souls. For my yoke is easy, and my burden is light." Matthew 11:28-30.

Lesson VII.

11. The will of God

"And this is the will of him, that sent me, that every one which seeth the Son, and believeth on him, may have everlasting life: and I will raise him up at the last day." John 6:40.

12. "Lord, to whom shall we go? Thou hast the words of eternal life." John 6:68.

Lesson VIII.

13. That which defiles

"Not that which goeth into the mouth defileth a man; but that which cometh out of the mouth, this defileth a man." Matthew 15:11.

Lesson IX.

14. How are we made free?

"And ye shall know the truth, and the truth shall make you free." John 8:32.

Lesson X.

15. Christ's teaching concerning covetousness

"Take heed, and beware of covetousness: for a man's life consisteth not in the abundance of the things which he possesseth." Luke 12:15.

Lesson XI.

16. Jesus, the promise of a new life

"I am the resurrection, and the life: he that believeth in me, though he were dead, yet shall he live." John 11:25.

Lesson XII.

17. Christ's measure of greatness

"But whosoever will be great among you, let him be your minister; And whosoever will be chief among you, let him be your servant: Even as the Son of man came not to be ministered unto, but to minister, and to give his life a ransom for many." Matthew 20:26-28.

Lesson XIII.

18. The Great Commandment

"Thou shalt love the Lord thy God with all thy heart, and with all thy soul, and with all thy mind. This is the first and great commandment. And the second is like unto it, Thou shalt love thy neighbor as thyself. On these two commandments hang all the law and the prophets." Matthew 22:37-40.

Lesson XIV.

19. How enduring is Christ's word?

"Heaven and earth shall pass away: but my words shall not pass away." Luke 21:33.

20. How can we minister to Christ?

"Inasmuch as ye have done it unto one of the least of these my brethren, ye have done it unto me." Matthew 25:40.

Lesson XV.

21. The importance of watching and praying

"Watch ye and pray, lest ye enter into temptation. The spirit truly is ready, but the flesh is weak." Mark 14:38.

22. Christ's consolation to believers

"Let not your heart be troubled: ye believe in God, believe also in me. In my Father's house are many mansions: If it were not so, I would have told you. I go to prepare a place for you. And if I go and prepare a place for you, I will come again, and receive you unto myself; that where I am, there ye may be also." John 14:1-3.

Lesson XVI.

23. The seven recorded sayings of Jesus on the cross

"Father, forgive them; for they know not what they do." Luke 23:34.

"Verily I say unto thee, Today shalt thou be with me in Paradise." Luke 23:43.

"Woman, behold thy son!" ... "Behold thy mother!" John 19:26, 27.

"My God, my God, why hast thou forsaken me?" Mark 15:34.

"I thirst." John 19:28.

"It is finished." John 19:30.

"Father, into thy hands I commend my spirit." Luke 23:46.

Lesson XVII.

24. The purpose of the Gospel

"But these are written, that ye may believe that Jesus is the Christ, the Son of God; and that believing ye might have life through his name." John 20:31.

Lesson XVIII.

25. What did Peter and the other apostles say when reprimanded by the high priest for preaching Christ?

"We ought to obey God rather than men." Acts 5:29.

Lesson XIX.

26. The beginning words of the first sermon to the Gentiles

"Of a truth I perceive that God is no respecter of persons: But in every nation he that feareth Him, and worketh righteousness, is accepted with Him." Acts 10:34, 35.

Lesson XXI.

27. For what were the people of Berea commended?

"These were more noble than those in Thessalonica, in that they received the word with all readiness of mind, and searched the scriptures daily, whether those things were so." Acts 17:11.

28. What does Acts 17:26 teach concerning the brotherhood of man?

"And God hath made of one blood all nations of men for to dwell on all the face of the earth, and hath determined the times before appointed, and the bounds of their habitation."

Lesson XXIII.

29. Why did Paul expect a crown of righteousness?

"I have fought a good fight, I have finished my course, I have kept the faith: Henceforth there is laid up for me a crown of righteousness, which the Lord, the righteous judge, shall give me at that day: and not to me only, but unto all them also that love His appearing." II Timothy 4:7, 8.

Lesson XXIV.

30. Good and evil

"Prove all things; hold fast that which is good. Abstain from all appearance of evil." I Thessalonians 5:21, 22.

Lesson XXVI.

31. The fruit of the Spirit

"But the fruit of the Spirit is love, joy, peace, longsuffering, gentleness, goodness, faith, meekness, temperance: against such there is no law." Galatians 5:22-23.

32. What may we expect to harvest?

"Be not deceived; God is not mocked: for whatsoever a man soweth, that shall he also reap." Galatians 6:7.

33. "Though I speak with the tongues of men and of angels, and have not charity, I am become as sounding brass, or a tinkling cymbal.

"And though I have the gift of prophecy, and understand all mysteries, and all knowledge; and though I have all faith, so that I could remove mountains, and have not charity, I am nothing.

"And though I bestow all my goods to feed the poor, and though I give my body to be burned, and have not charity, it profiteth me nothing.

"Charity suffereth long, and is kind; charity envieth not; charity vaunteth not itself, is not puffed up,

"Doth not believe itself unseemly, seeketh not her own, is not easily provoked, thinketh no evil;

"Rejoiceth not in iniquity, but rejoiceth in the truth;

"Beareth all things, believeth all things, hopeth all things, endureth all things.

"Charity never faileth: but whether there be prophecies, they shall fail; whether there be tongues, they shall cease; whether there be knowledge, it shall vanish away.

"For we know in part, and we prophesy in part.

"But when that which is perfect is come, then that which is in part shall be done away.

"When I was a child, I spake as a child, I understood as a child, I thought as a child: but when I became a man, I put away childish things.

"For now we see through a glass darkly; but then face to face: now I know in part; but then I shall know even as also I am known.

"And now abideth faith, hope, charity, these three; but the greatest of these is charity." I Corinthians 13.

Lesson XXIX.

34. The penalty for sin and the gift of God contrasted

"For the wages of sin is death; but the gift of God is eternal life through Jesus Christ our Lord." Romans 6:23.

35. Reasonable service

"I beseech you therefore, brethren, by the mercies of God, that ye present your bodies a living sacrifice, holy, acceptable unto God, which is your reasonable service. And be not conformed to this world: but be ye transformed by the renewing of your mind, that ye may prove what is that good, and acceptable, and perfect, will of God." Romans 12:1, 2.

Lesson XXXII.

36. Upon what should Christians meditate?

"Finally, brethren, whatsoever things are true, whatsoever things are honest, whatsoever things are just, whatsoever things are pure, whatsoever things are lovely, whatsoever things are of good report; if there be any virtue, and if there be any praise,think on these things." Philippians 4:8.

Lesson XXXIV.

37. Faith defined

"Now faith is the substance of things hoped for, the evidence of things not seen." Hebrews 11:1.

Lesson XXXVI.

38. What must we do besides hear?

"But be ye doers of the word, and not hearers only, deceiving your own selves." James 1:22.

Lesson XXXVIII.

39. The importance of study

"Study to show thyself approved unto God, a workman that needeth not to be ashamed, rightly dividing the word of truth." II Timothy 2:15.

40. Value of the scriptures

"All scripture is given by inspiration of God, and is profitable for doctrine, for reproof, for correction, for instruction in righteousness:

"That the man of God may be perfect, thoroughly furnished unto all good works." II Timothy 3:16-17.

Lesson XLIV

41. What virtues are Christians exhorted to add to their faith?

"Giving all diligence, add to your faith virtue; and to virtue knowledge; And to knowledge temperance; and to temperance patience; and to patience godliness; And to godliness brotherly kindness; and to brotherly kindness charity. For these things be in you, and abound, they make you that ye shall neither be barren nor unfruitful in the knowledge of our Lord Jesus Christ." II Peter 1:5-8.

Lesson XLV

42. A promise to the faithful

"Be thou faithful unto death, and I will give thee a crown of life." Revelation 2:10.

THE PARABLES OF JESUS
(Selected List)*

THE PARABLE	WHERE RECORDED				THE LEADING LESSON
	MATT.	MARK	LUKE		
1. New Wine in Old Bottles	9:17	2:22	5:37		New spirit in unregenerate hearts.
2. The Sower	13:3	4:3	8:5		The different classes of hearers.
3. The Tares	13:24				Good and evil not separated in this life.
4. The Barren Fig Tree			13:9		Fruitfulness required.
5. The Mustard Seed	13:31	4:30	13:18		The small beginning of Christ's Kingdom.
6. The Seed Growing Secretly		4:26			The law of development.
7. The Leaven	13:33		13:20		The pervading influence of Christ's gospel.
8. The Hid Treasure	13:44				The value of the Kingdom.
9. The Goodly Pearl	13:45				The Kingdom worth more than all things.
10. The Fisherman's Net	13:47				The visible church gathers good and bad.
11. The Good Samaritan			10:30		Active benevolence.
12. The Importunate Friend			11:5		Perseverance in prayer.
13. The Rich Fool			12:16		Worldy mindness and ambition.
14. The Great Supper			14:16		Universality of the divine call.
15. The Two Sons	21:28				Insincerity and repentance.
16. The Prodigal Son			15:11		Fatherly love for the returning sinner.
17. The Unjust Steward			16:1		Faithfulness to trust in little things.
18. The Pharisee and the Publican			18:10		Self-righteousness and humility.
19. The Pounds			19:12		Diligence rewarded; selfishness punished.
20. The Ten Virgins	25:1				Preparedness.
21. The Talents	25:14				Use of opportunity.

*Pupils should be held responsible for the list of parables given in this chart. Teachers and pupils are expected to place their own interpretation on the teachings of the parables.

MIRACLES OF JESUS

*(Selected List, Robertson's Harmony)**

THE MIRACLE	WHERE RECORDED			
	MATT.	MARK	LUKE	JOHN
1. *Water Turned into Wine				2:1-11
2. *Healing Nobleman's Son				4:46-54
3. First Draught of Fishes			5:6	
4. Demoniac in the Synagogue		1:26	4:35	
5. *Peter's Mother-in-Law Healed	8:14	1:31	4:39	
6. A Leper Cleansed	8:3	1:41	5:13	
7. *Paralytic Healed	9:2	2:3	5:18	
8. Impotent Man Healed				5:5
9. Man with a Withered Hand	12:10	3:1	6:6	
10. Centurion's Servant Healed	8:5	7:2		
11. Widow's Son Raised			7:11	
12. Blind and Dumb Man Healed	12:22			
13. *Tempest Stilled		4:39	8:24	
14. Demoniacs of Sadara	8:28	5:1	8:26	
15. Woman with Issue of Blood Cured	9:20	5:25	8:43	
16. Daughter of Jairus Raised	9:18	5:42	8:41	
17. Two Blind Men Healed	9:27			
18. A Dumb Demoniac Healed	9:32			
19. *Feeding of the Five Thousand	14:15	6:41	9:12	6:5
20. *Walking on the Sea	14:25	6:49		6:19
21. Daughter of Syrophenician	15:22	7:25		
22. Deaf and Dumb Healed		7:33		
23. Feeding of the Four Thousand	15:32	8:8		
24. Blind Man of Bethsaida Healed		8:23		
25. Demoniac Boy Healed	17:18	9:25	9:43	
26. Tribute Money	17:24-27			
27. Man Born Blind Healed				9:7
28. Woman with Spirit of Infirmity Healed			13:11	
29. Man with Dropsy			14:2	
30. *Lazarus Raised				11:1-44
31. The Ten Lepers			17:12	
32. *Blind Bartimeus	20:30	10:49	18:40	
33. Barren Fig Tree Cursed	21:19			
34. *Ear of High Priest's Servant (Malchus) Restored			22:50-51	18:10
35. Second Draught of Fishes				21:6

*This list of miracles is given chiefly for reference and review purposes. Students should be held responsible for knowing the setting and meaning of the most commonly known miracles, such as those starred.

SPECIMEN EXAMINATION QUESTIONS
FINAL EXAMINATION IN NEW TESTAMENT
MAY 11, 1946

Name_____Address_____Phone_____

Church_____S. S. Teacher_____

High School_____Have you kept an approved notebook?_____

Are you a contestant for the Linz Award?___Year in High School____

Answer all 10 of the division questions, omitting such optional number in each as is indcated.

I—Value 10 (1 each)

Give the names of three large parts or divisions, of the New Testament Course of Study, and place *any* 7 of the following items opposite the correct part: (1) Pentecost, (2) Stephen's death, (3) Shipwreck of Paul, (4) Beatitudes, (5) Missionary journeys, (6) Philip the deacon, (7) John the Baptist, (8) Transfiguration, (9) Romans. Write the *number* of the item and not the item itself.

          Name of Part   *Items*

Part One_____   _____

Part Two_____   _____

Part Three_____   _____

II—Value 10

(a) Complete any 8 of the following quotations: (Value 4 —½ each)

  1. "Be ye doers_____."

  2. "God is no_____."

  3. "Be thou faithful_____."

  4. "I am the_____."

  5. "Wist ye not_____."

  6. "Be not deceived_____."

  7. "Thou shall call_____."

  8. "The wages_____."

  9. "Man shall not_____."

(b) Quote in full the: Golden Rule (Value 1).

(c) Quote in full five Beatitudes (Value 5).

III—Value 10 (1 each)

In any of the blanks below write the *number* of the parable in the second column which best matches the thought expressed in the first column. The first blank is filled out correctly to show what is meant.

(11) Fruitfulness required.	1.	The ten virgins.
—— Value of Kingdom.	2.	The sower.
—— Law of development.	3.ˋ	The leaven.
—— Universality of the divine call.	4.	The great supper.
—— Self righteousness and humility.	5.	The seed growing secretly.
—— Good and evil not separated in this life.	6.	The hid treasure.
—— Preparedness.	7.	The good Samaritan.
—— Pervading influence of Christ's gospel.	8.	The talents.
—— Active benevolence.	9.	The two sons.
—— The small beginning of Christ's Kingdom.	10.	The Pharisee and the Publican.
—— Classes of hearers.	11.	The barren fig tree.
—— Insincerity and repentance.	12.	The mustard seed.
—— Use of opportunity.	13.	The tares.

IV—Value 10 (½ each)

Complete any 20 of the following concerning the life of Paul.

1. He was born in the city of_____.
2. By race he was_____.
3. By citizenship he was_____.
4. He was educated for the work of_____.
5. He persecuted early Christians in_____.
6. He was converted and stricken_____.
7. He was the great "missionary to the_____."
8. He and Barnabas were sent out from_____ on a missionary journey.
9. He made_____missionary journeys into Asia.
10. His companions on the second journey were_____ and_____.
11. He wrote letters to two young preachers,_____ and_____.
12. A call for help came to him from_____.

13. He attended the great council at_____.
14. His first European convert was a_____.
15. His first European Church was founded at_____.
16. Another convert there was the_____.
17. He founded other churches at_____
    and_____.
18. He wrote_____of the Epistles (letters).
19. He was shipwrecked on his journey to_____.
20. He was imprisioned two years in_____.
21. His beloved physician was_____.
22. He preached the gospel to the_____first.

V—Value 10 (½ each)

Write a check mark (√) in the proper blank for any 20 of the following to show whether statement is true or false. An example is given to show what is meant.

	True	False	
	√	___	Christ chose twelve apostles.
1.	___	___	John the Baptist was the forerunner of Christ.
2.	___	___	There are only two gospels.
3.	___	___	Mark's Gospel was written to the Jews.
4.	___	___	Moses and Elias were present at the Transfiguration.
5.	___	___	The Holy Ghost came at Pentecost.
6.	___	___	Much is known of Jesus' childhood.
7.	___	___	There are many rivers in Palestine.
8.	___	___	Ananias was striken dead for lying to the Holy Ghost.
9.	___	___	The Sermon on the Mount is found in Mark.
10.	___	___	The Prodigal Son did not return to his father.
11.	___	___	Judas met death by the hand of others.
12.	___	___	Nine of the ten lepers cleansed returned to thank Christ.
13.	___	___	Christ was alone at His ascension.
14.	___	___	God and the Holy Spirit manifested themselves at Christ's baptism.
15.	___	___	Satan tempted Christ three times.

16. ____ ____ The Dead Sea is below sea-level.
17. ____ ____ Revelation is a prophetical book.
18. ____ ____ Barnabas went on a missionary journey with Paul.
19. ____ ____ Christ worshipped and taught in the synagogue.
20. ____ ____ Thomas was the only apostle at the Transfiguration.
21. ____ ____ Christ quoted the Scriptures in reply to Satan's temptations.
22. ____ ____ Christ discussed the "new birth" with Nicodemus.

VI—Value 10 (1 each)

Name 5 different authors of "Letters and Revelation," and give one book each wrote.

	Author	Book
1.	_____	_____
2.	_____	_____
3.	_____	_____
4.	_____	_____
5.	_____	_____

VII—Value 10 (1 each)

In any 10 of the blanks below write the *number* of the item in the second column which best matches the thought expressed in the first column. The first blank is filled out correctly to show what is meant.

_5_	Faith and works.	1. John.
____	History of early church.	2. I Thessalonians.
____	Most prominent religious sect.	3. Cana.
____	A tax collector.	4. Jerusalem.
____	Disbelief in the resurrection.	5. James.
____	Christ's first miracle.	6. Antioch.
____	Pentecost.	7. Bethlehem.
____	Paul's first letter.	8. Anointed One.
____	Beloved disciple.	9. Jewish Court.
____	First called "Christians."	10. Publican.
____	Messiah.	11. Pharisees.
____	Sanhedrin.	12. Sadducees.
		13. Acts.

VIII—Value 10 (½ each)

(a) Write in the blanks the *number* of the *correct term* in any of the following. An example is given to show what is meant.

(2)   Jesus spent the greater part of His childhood in: (1) Bethlehem. (2) Nazareth, (3) Capernaum.

1. _____ The parable teaching worldly ambition is: (1) (1) The talents, (2) The goodly pearl, (3) Rich fool.

2. _____ Christ stilled the storm on: (1) The Dead Sea, (2) The Sea of Galilee, (3) Mediterranean Sea.

3. _____ The gift acceptable to Christ was made by: (1) The Pharisee, (2) The Publican, (3) The widow.

4. _____ The "Missionary to the Gentiles" was: (1) Luke, (2) Paul, (3) Titus.

5. _____ The rivers of Palestine are: (1) Nile, (2) Euphrates, (3) Jordan.

6. _____ A brother of Christ was: (1) James, (2) Andrew, (3) Philip.

7. _____ Christ was betrayed by: (1) Barnabas, (2) Titus, (3) Judas.

8. _____ The mother of Christ was: (1) Martha, (2) Mary, (3) Lydia.

9. _____ Paul wrote two letters to a young preacher: (1) Pilate, (2) Nicodemus, (3) Timothy.

10. _____ At the time of Christ, Palestine was under the power of: (1) Rome, (2) Greece, (3) Egypt.

11. _____ The first church in Europe was established at: (1) Ephesus, (2) Philippi, (3) Athens.

(b) Write in the blanks the *number* of the *incorrect term* in any 10 of the following.

1. _____ Christ's miracles were called: (1) Signs, (2) Wonders, (3) Parables.

2. _____ The events of Passion week were: (1) Christ's trial, (2) The Crucifixion, (3) Baptism.

3. _____ The twelve chosen by Jesus were called: (1) disciples, (2) apostles, (3) scribes.

4. _____ The Synoptic Gospels are: (1) Matthew, (2) Luke, (3) John.

5. _____ Christ said seek first: (1) Kindom of God, (2) righteousness, (3) glory.

6. _____ Christ was tried before: (1) Herod, (2) Pilate, (3) Joseph.

7. _____ Christ raised from the dead: (1) Lazarus, (2) Daughter of Jairus, (3) Lydia.

8. _____ New testament books written by John are: (1) Gospel, (2) Revelation, (3) Acts.

9. _____ Paul's writings are called: (1) epistles, (2) letters, (3) manuscripts.

10. _____ After His resurrection, Christ appeared to: (1) Mary Magdalene, (2) Luke, (3) Peter.

11. _____ Letters written by Paul are: (1) Jude, (2) Ephesians, (3) Galatians.

IX—Value 10 (2 each)

Quote accurately the passages of Scripture which tell:

1. The purpose of Christ's coming.—John 3:16.

2. The value of the study of the Scriptures.—2 Tim. 2:15.

3. The purpose of the Gospel.—John 20:31.

4. Things that abide.—I Cor. 13:13.

5. The three-fold purpose of prayer.—Mt. 7:7.

X—Value 10 (1 each)

On the map given below, locate any 10 of the following by writing in the proper place on the map the *number* (figure) placed in *front* of each term: (1) Sea of Galilee, (2) Dead Sea, (3) Bethlehem, (4) Nazareth, (5) Jerusalem, (6) Jericho (7) Jordan River, (8) Tyre, (9) Mt. Hermon, (10) Capernaum, (11) the three chief divisions of Palestine in New Testament times. For number (11) draw boundary lines and write names of divisions.

GLOSSARY

Advocate. One who pleads for another.

Almighty. All-powerful.

Alms. Something given as charity, whether in goods or money.

Amen. "So be it."

Anchor. That which holds fast.

Antichrist. Opponent of Christ.

Apocalypse. Revelation.

Apostle. One sent forth.

Appoint. To assign, to allot, to ordain, to set apart.

Areopagus. An Athenian court on Mar's Hill in Athens where Paul preached.

Authority. Right to govern.

Barbarian. According to the Greeks, "Every one not a Greek."

Beatitude. A declaration of blessedness; state of being blessed; the abiding satisfaction and profound joy one finds in living as God desires him to live.

Benediction. Good words; the act of blessing.

Believe. To trust, to rely on, to accept, to obey.

Betray. To give up faithlessly; to deliver to the power of the enemy.

Betroth. To promise in marriage.

Bible. "The Book."

Blasphemy. Irreverent words; speaking evil of God.

Buffet. To strike, to slap.

Calvary. (Greek) The place where Jesus was crucified. (See Golgotha)

Centurion. A Roman officer of a hundred men.

Chaste. Consecrated, pure, virtuous.

Christian. A follower of Christ; the disciples were first called Christians at Antioch of Syria; they were known to each other as the "brethren."

Comforter. The Holy Spirit.

Confirm. To strengthen, to make firm, to establish.

Conversation. Behavior, conduct, talk.

Council. An assembly for consultation.

Counsel. (verb) To advise; (noun), advice.

Covenant. Will, agreement, testament; the Old Testament is the old agreement between God and man; the New Testament is the new pact that was made with God.

Covet. To crave or desire something belonging to another.

Crown. Emblem of royalty.

Crucify. To kill by nailing to a tree or cross.

Damnation. Condemnation.

Deacon. A Church official whose duties were various and indiscriminate. The office of the deacon was lower than that of the apostles, yet the demand for moral refinement, holy living, and consistent character were on the same level.

Decrees. Authoritative decisions.

Despise. To reject; to lightly esteem.

Devout. Reverential; zealous in attachment.

Diana. Goddess of the Ephesians, an idol believed to have fallen down from heaven.

Disciple. Learner, follower.

Discourse. Conversation.

Dispensation. Bestowment, an appointed order or system.

Dispersion. Those Jews who remained in foreign countries after the Babylonian exile.

Divination. False systems or methods of learning the divine will.

Emulation. Ambition to excell; jealous rivalry.

Epistle. Letter, especially the Apostolic letter.

Exhort. To urge to good deeds.

Exorcist. One who pretended to expel evil spirits.

Expedient. Advisable, profitable.

Feast of Dedication. Instituted by Judas Maccabaeus, B.C. 164, at the time of the purifying of the Temple and rebuilding of the altar after their pollution by Antiochus Epiphanes, observed on the 25th of Kisleu (December). It has been called the "Feast of Lights."

Gainsay. To deny, to dispute, to oppose.

Gentile. Any person not of the Jewish race; a Greek.

Golgotha. (Hebrew) The place where Jesus was crucified (See Calvary)

Gospel. Good news; the teachings of Christ.

Grecian. A Jew by birth or religion who spoke Greek; a Hellenist.

Hallelujah. "Praise ye Jehovah."

Haply. Perhaps, by chance.

Heresy. Doctrine not in harmony with Holy Scriptures.

Honor. Reverence, worship, regard, glory.

Hope. (verb) To desire and expect; (noun) confident expectation.

Hosanna. "Save, we pray."

Husks. Fruit of a variety of locust tree, used as food by the poor and for feeding hogs.

Idol. Anything used as an object of worship in place of the true God.

Idolatry. The worship of idols.

Immanuel. "God is with us!" The promised Messiah.

Immortal. Everlasting, not subject to death.

Impotent. Powerless, weak.

Importunate. Troublesome, urgent or persistent in solicitation.

Inspiration. "Breathed into," divine influence, divine direction.

Intent. Design, purpose.

Jesus. "Jehovah is salvation."

Justify. To defend, to make just.

Keep. Observe, heed, protect, preserve.

Leper. Sufferer from leprosy.

Leprosy. Loathsome and severe skin disease.

Malefactor. Evildoer, criminal.

Malice. Ill-will, spite, grudge.

Martyr. One dying for his faith.

Meet. Sufficient, right, suitable, fit.

Messiah. "Anointed one;" the looked-for king and deliverer of the Jews; "Chosen one of God."

Millstone. Stone used for grinding grain.

Miracle. That which surpasses human or natural powers; the "signs," "works," "wonders," and "powers" that identified Christ as the Messiah.

Mote. A speck; a very small thing.

Nurture. Care; education.

Offend. To sin against, to cause to stumble.

Oracles. Messages of God.

Ordinance. A law or command of God.

Parable. (A placing side by side) A short story designed to convey some important truth by comparison; an earthly story with a heavenly meaning.

Passion. Suffering.

Passover. An annual Jewish spring feast commemorating two events: the sparing of the firstborn when God smote the Egyptians and their deliverance from Egyptian bondage.

Peculiar. Particular, individual, separated from others, different.

Pentecost, The Feast of. The second of the annual feasts, observed in June, commemorating the giving of the Law on Mt. Sinai. It was celebrated fifty days after the Passover.

Pervert. To turn from right.

Pharisees. Jewish sect noted for self-righteousness, formalism, and hypocrisy. They accepted and emphasized oral traditions of their fathers, as well as the law, as binding.

Philosophy. Earthly wisdom.

Prevent. To come before, to hinder.

Profane. Not sacred; irreverent, blasphemous.

Prophesy. (verb) To foretell, with divine inspiration.

Proselyte. Foreigner who adopted the Jewish religion.

Publican. Tax collector for the Roman government.

Quick. Having life, speedy.

Rabbi. Jewish teacher or doctor of the Law.

Rabboni. "My Master and my Father;" title of highest respect.

Reconciliation. The act of restoring friendship or favor after estrangement.

Redeem. To save from being lost, to buy back.

Remission. Pardon, forgiveness.

Reprobate. Wicked, corrupt.

Sackcloth and ashes. Used to denote humiliation and extreme grief.

Sadducees. An aristocratic Jewish Sect, influential politically. They opposed the Pharisees. They rejected the traditions of the elders, accepting only the written law as binding. They denied the resurrection, immortality, and the existence of angels and spirits.

Saint. One set apart, a godly person.

Salvation. Redemption from sin.

Samaritans. A mixed group of Assyrian and Jewish people, in the time of our Lord. The hatred between the Jews and the Samaritans was still so bitter that the Galileans, when going up to Jerusalem, avoided passing through Samaria.

Sanhedrin. The highest Jewish Court composed of seventy-one members (Pharisees, Sadducees, priests, and scribes). This court served in Jerusalem trying cases pertaining to Jewish matters. Twenty-three formed a quorum.

Scribes. Those who copied, taught, and explained the Jewish law; the lawyers.

Scripture. Written revelation from God.

Similitude. Resemblance.

Strait. Narrow, difficult.

Straightway. Immediately.

Subvert. Corrupt, pervert.

Synagogue. Jewish house of worship, school, court, and general meetings.

Tare. A weed, especially one in Palestine that closely resembled wheat before the ear was formed.

Temple. The sacred edifice in Jerusalem that was the religious center of the Jewish nation.

Testament. Will, covenant, agreement.

Traditions. Beliefs, opinions, customs handed down from generation to generation by word of mouth or practice.

Transfiguration. A change in outward form or appearance; Christ was visibly glorified at His transfiguration.

Worship. Pay divine honor to; adoring reverence for.

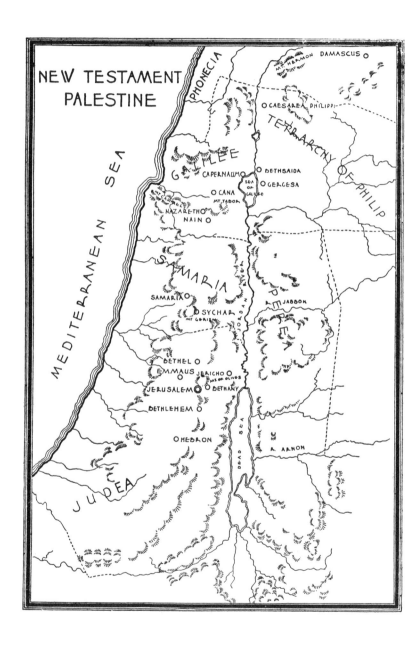

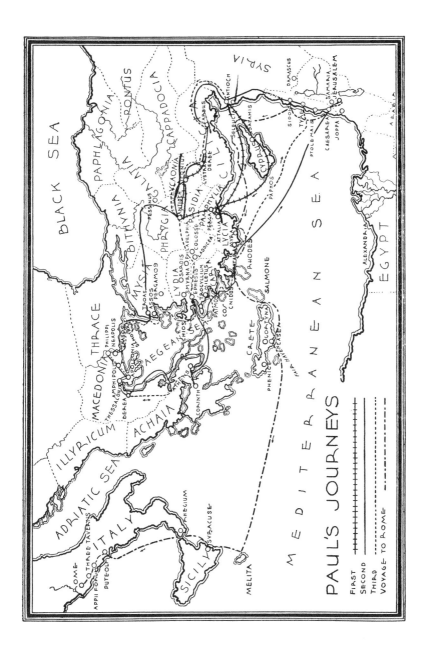

Price List

Prices subject to change without notice
Quantity and case-lot discounts available

WallBuilders, Inc.
P.O. Box 397
Aledo, TX 76008
(817) 441-6044

	Price/Copy	Quantity	Total
Books & Publications			
America: To Pray or Not To Pray?	$6.95	_____	___
A statistical look at what has happened when religious principles were separated from public affairs by the Supreme Court in 1962 and at what can be done to repair the damage to the nation.			
The Myth of Separation	$7.95	_____	___
An examination of the writings of the Framers of the Constitution and of the Supreme Court's own records proving that the separation of church and state is a recent innovation in America having no precedent in American history or legal practice.			
The Bulletproof George Washington	$4.95	_____	___
Until 1934, this account of God's miraculous protection of Washington in the French and Indian War and of his open gratitude for God's Divine intervention could be found in virtually all student textbooks.			
The New England Primer	$5.95	_____	___
A reprint of the 1777 textbook used by the Founding Fathers. The *Primer* was the first textbook ever printed in America (Boston, 1690) and was used to teach reading and Bible lessons in schools for over 200 years.			
What Happened in Education?	$2.95	_____	___
Statistical evidence that disproves several popular educational explanations for the decline in SAT scores.			
Did Television Cause the Changes in Youth Morality?	$2.95	_____	___
An examination to determine if TV caused the declines in youth morality that began in 1963. The results are very enlightening not only as to what happened in television, but when it happened, and why?			
Cassette Tapes			
"America's Godly Heritage" (See video)	$4.95	_____	___
"Education and the Founding Fathers" (See Video)	$4.95	_____	___
"The Spirit of the American Revolution"	$4.95	_____	___
A look at the Christian motivation of the Founders throughout the American Revolution.			
"The Laws of the Heavens"	$4.95	_____	___
An explanation of the eight words in the Declaration of Independence on which the nation was birthed.			
"America: Lessons from Nehemiah"	$4.95	_____	___

A look at the scriptural parallels between the
rebuilding of Jerusalem in the book of Nehemiah
and that of America today.

"The Founding Fathers"	$4.95	_____ _____

Highlights accomplishments and notable quotes
of prominent Founding Fathers which show their
strong belief in Christian principles.

"Keys to Good Government"	$4.95	_____ _____

The Founding Fathers formula for good government.

"8 Principles for Reformation"	$4.95	_____ _____

Eight Biblical guidelines for restoring Christian
principles to society and public affairs.

"The Myth of Separation" (See book)	$4.95	_____ _____
"America: To Pray or Not To Pray" (See book)	$4.95	_____ _____

eo Cassette (VHS)

America's Godly Heritage (60 min.)	$19.95	_____ _____

This clearly sets forth the beliefs of many of the
famous Founding Fathers concerning the proper
role of Christian principles in education,
government, and the public affairs of the nation.

Education and the Founding Fathers (60 min.)	$19.95	_____ _____

A look at the Bible-based educational system
which produced America's great heroes and what
they said and did (in their writings, laws, and
Court decisions) to ensure that America would
always continue to have that same Christian
system of education.

Foundations of American Government (18 min.)	$9.95	_____ _____

Surveys the historical statements and records
surrounding the original drafting of the First
Amendment and what has happened statistically
since the 1962 Court rejected the Founders' intent.

Tax (TX only, add 7.75%): _____

Shipping (see chart at left): _____

TOTAL: _____

Shipping and Handling

Jnder $5.00	$1.50	$25.01-$ 40.00	$5.95
5.01-$15.00	$2.95	$40.01-$ 60.00	$6.95
15.01-$25.00	$3.95	$60.01-$100.00	$9.95

Canada orders add $5 extra.

Send The Above Indicated Materials To:

ne_____Phone ( )_____

lress_____

_____State_____Zip_____

"You see the distress that we are in . . . come, let us build the walls
that we may no longer be a reproach." Nehemiah 2:17.